This reference book is made available in accordance with a plan promulgated under the requirements of Section 14, Subdivision VIII of the liquor law. This plan provides for collaboration between the School Authorities and the Liquor Control Board of the State of Vermont.

REGINALD T. COLE,

Liquor Administrator

ALCOHOL

and the

Habit-Forming Drugs

By

GRANT L. DONNELLY, A.B. in Educ., M.D.

ASSOCIATE PROFESSOR OF PHARMACOLOGY, THE MEDICAL SCHOOL,
UNIVERSITY OF NORTH CAROLINA

Illustrations by

MARY DEB. GRAVES

Chapel Hill, North Carolina

ALFRED WILLIAMS & COMPANY

PUBLISHERS

RALEIGH, NORTH CAROLINA

PREFACE

The object of this little volume is to make available
for school children of an appropriate age, an honest
and therefore an unbiased statement based on certain
facts concerning the action of alcohol, the alcoholic
beverages and certain drugs which may be classed as
habit-forming substances such as the narcotics. No
attempt has been made to conduct a crusade against
the use of the alcoholic beverages. It falls, however,
within both the scope and object of this volume to
point out their deleterious influence, the ease with
which a habit may be developed for them and their
well nigh lack of value as remedial agents. The author
has accomplished this object in a clear, easily under-
standable and fair fashion. In addition to having at-
tained this major objective, he has outlined in a most
attractive manner the way in which alcohol is produced and has shown the influence of this substance
on human beings as individuals and collectively
through them on society. In addition, he has indicated
the enormous value of alcohol to various industries
and in this way the significant part it assumes eco-
omically.

Closely related to the action of alcohol, the desire
or it, and an addiction to its use, are certain habit-
orming drugs generally spoken of as the narcotics.

In addition to these major narcotic substances such as opium and its various preparations, hashish, heroin and cocaine there are a number of drugs which cannot be classed as narcotics but which have an influence on the central nervous system as useful drugs in certain diseased states but when taken with the freedom which their sale permits may render in part ineffective this important system of the body and cause changes of degeneration in other tissues. Substances such as veronal, luminal in its various forms, aspirin, the bromides and acetanilid should be looked upon as useful drugs, which, in overdoses, are severely acting poisons. As has been indicated so clearly in this text, these substances should be used with very great caution and had best be prescribed by a physician.

Innately honest and fair, fundamentally trained in educational psychology and later in the biological sciences and in medicine, Dr. Donnelly has made through these attributes a contribution to the school curriculum which gives in a happy and an accurate fashion to young people and children an understanding of extremely important information.

WM. DEB. MACNIDER
The Laboratory of Pharmacology
The University of North Carolina
July 6, 1936

CONTENTS

LIST OF ILLUSTRATIONS

FOREWORD TO THE TEACHER

The use of alcohol has been and still is a controversial subject based on moral issues and the rights of the individual. The approach to the problem here is on the basis of scientific truth rather than morals and personal rights. Your reaction to the teaching of this subject may not be in accord with your formed opinions. Such opinions will not, however, alter the feeling of responsibility on the part of the honest teacher. You are well aware of the pliability of the child mind and how long moulded impressions may last. All of us remember the teacher influences in our own lives, some of them empty and some of them full to the brim with hopes, dreams and ambitions. We are attempting to treat our subject from a new and different angle, to a different group of individuals. This new approach is an experiment, but it seems to be a logical and reasonable one. Its possibilities are good but its success depends on the interested teacher who is willing to give it a fair and honest trial. The method of application is, of course, left to the ingenuity of the trained teacher of the proper grade level.

The use of alcohol and the habit-forming drugs has become more than a problem of morals and rights. With a large percentage of the adult and near adult population addicted to the use of alcohol and other drugs, there is created a health problem which threatens to become a serious influence for the future. When we add to this the social consequences depending largely on health factors, the dangers become more apparent.

Production, we are told, is based on the law of demand. In this country such a law controls the production of beverage alcohol and certain drugs. At its foundation the law as applied here is faulty because it is not based on a knowledge of the after effects of these substances on health. Make that knowledge universal in an honest, unbiased manner, and in time good results are bound to come. It may take ten or twenty years but the results will be worth the wait.

G. L. D.

Unit I.

THE STORY OF ALCOHOL

---

1. Early History of Alcohol.
2. What is Alcohol?
3. How is Alcohol Made?
4. How is Alcohol Used?

THE STORY OF ALCOHOL

Do you like history and chemistry?

You sit at comfortable desks, in well lighted, well heated rooms. Your books are well printed and filled with interesting pictures. Thousands of years ago, there were no modern conveniences, and living was not easy. People knew nothing about history and chemistry. In the section to follow, you will learn something about how, under very difficult conditions, the writing of history began. You will learn how some of the natural chemical processes were used by people who did not understand what was happening. You will see how one of these early chemical processes produced a substance of great value; how it is made; and how it is used today.

EARLY HISTORY OF ALCOHOL

A great American once said, "beginnings keep no records." We know that people lived in the world long before the writing of history began. No records were kept, probably because there was no way to keep them. Finally, as civilization moved ahead, someone realized that the people of the future would like to know what had gone on in the early, uncertain days of the beginning. Perhaps with such a thought in mind, the Egyptians, nearly six thousand years ago, first started the written story of civilization. The Egyptians had no paper, pens, or printing presses. They could not write books like the ones we study. Their task was indeed a difficult one. In the place of paper they used flat stones. On these stones were carved pictures and word symbols or signs. Of course, there were no libraries in which to keep the queer stone pages, so that in time many of them were destroyed or lost. Some of the carvings were placed in the tombs of the kings. These tombs, or burying places, have since been opened and the carved stones recovered. By studying the symbols and pictures, a great deal has been learned about how the Egyptians of that period lived and what they did.

(Adapted from the Standard Encyclopedia of the Alcohol Problem. Courtesy of the American Issue Pub. Co.)

Early Egyptian stone carvings showing vineyard, footpress, and wine drinking.

From some of the later records, carved about five thousand years ago, we have the first mention of an alcoholic drink, called beer. The beer was made from some kind of sprouted grain. Beer was made in Egypt because Egypt was rich in grain and poor in fruits. You will recall from Biblical history that Joseph's brothers, during a period of famine, went down into Egypt to buy grain, since grain was plentiful there.

Perhaps, with the very beginning of civilization, wine containing alcohol was made quite by accident when souring fruit juice was left standing in rough stone vessels or skin bags.

In ancient times, the people living around the Mediterranean Sea grew many grapes, figs, and other fruits. It was natural, then, that the making of wine should begin with them. In the Bible many stories are told about the making and drinking of wine. About four thousand years ago, Noah, who built the Ark, was the first man recorded in history to get drunk on wine. He was also the first man to plant a vineyard and, probably, the first to develop the art of making wine. It must have been a common occurrence for people of that time to get drunk, because Noah's son was punished for laughing at his father's drunken condition. This, of course, meant that the son had seen people in that condition before and knew how they were affected. If you saw a drunken man for the first time, you might think that he was very sick. Instead of laughing at him, you would probably try to get a doctor.

One thousand years after Noah lived, Moses described the wine of Israel's enemies as "the poison of dragons and the cruel venom of asps." Still later, wine drinking was described as being very widespread. At the feasts of King Belshazzar much wine was consumed and usually all of the people became drunk.

From the oldest records of China we know that wine making and drinking were common. One kind of wine was made from fermented rice. It is recalled in an old story that a Chinese emperor had all the grape vineyards pulled up by the roots so that his people could not make wine.

Alcohol and water are not so much alike as they look.

WHAT IS ALCOHOL?

Pure alcohol is a chemical substance which looks exactly like water. If we filled one glass with water and another glass with alcohol, we could not tell any difference between the two by looking at them. Since

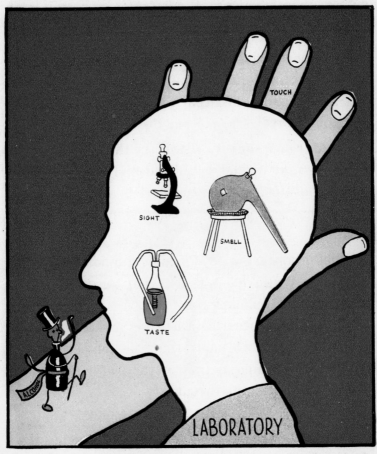

Alcohol enters the laboratories of sight, taste, smell and touch.

alcohol and water look alike, how can we tell them
apart? We can take them into our laboratories and
make some simple tests which will show us a great
deal of difference between the two. But you may ask,
where are our laboratories? All of us have very fine

laboratories which we are using every minute of the day for many purposes.

Our laboratories are our senses of sight, hearing, smell, taste, and touch. We have already made the first test and have learned that alcohol looks like water and not like molasses.

Now for another test. Let us try the sense of smell. First, we take up the water and find it has no odor. How about the alcohol? Yes, here is a big difference. Alcohol has a strong but pleasant odor, somewhat like perfume.

What other tests can we make? Suppose we try the taste test. Water has no taste that we can describe, but it certainly makes the inside of the mouth feel good. Alcohol has a sweet taste and makes the mouth feel warm. Yet we know that the temperature of alcohol is the same as that of the water. Alcohol is strong and burns the throat.

Here is another good test—the touch. We know, of course, how our skin feels when water touches it. If the hands are wet with alcohol, the skin feels slick and very cool. Alcohol evaporates or dries almost at once so that the hands are soon dry.

Other tests show that alcohol is lighter than water. It will burn like gasoline and gives a blue flame without smoke.

Here is a picture of the process of fermentation. Carbon dioxide comes
out in the form of gas bubbles, and alcohol stays in the water.

What a big difference our laboratory tests have
shown. We can see by now that alcohol is not so much
like water as our first sight test indicated.

HOW IS ALCOHOL MADE?

Fermentation. (fûr′-mĕn-ta′shŭn)—Alcohol is
formed by a process we call **fermentation**. Fermentation is a big word, but it simply means to boil. This is
not the same kind of boiling that takes place in the
kettle of water on the hot stove. It is "boiling" caused
by yeast cells.

When yeast, sugar and water get together fermentation takes place and alcohol is formed.

Here is another way for you to make a test. This time it will be on fermentation and you can do a real experiment like the ones done in the laboratory.

Get a small piece of baking yeast, about the size of your thumb, and a half-dozen tablespoonfuls of sugar. Dissolve the sugar and yeast in a half-gallon jar full of water. Put the jar in a warm place and look at it several times a day. Soon you will see bubbles coming to the top of the water. These bubbles rise as the bubbles do in boiling water. A long, long time ago people saw this same thing happening in fruit juice. It reminded them of the bubbles in boiling water, so they gave it the **Latin** name fermentation, from **fervere**, which means to boil.

What causes the bubbles to rise in the water? First, do you know what yeast is? In the cake which comes from the grocery store, yeast looks somewhat like dried dough. In that small cake of yeast there are millions and millions of little round plant cells. In the dry cake they cannot grow, but that does not mean they are dead. Yeast cells, like all living things, must have food and water before they can grow. The yeast cells in the jar get their food from the sugar water. New yeast cells grow out as buds on the old yeast plants. These buds grow somewhat as buds grow out from a limb. The bud on a yeast plant soon breaks off to become a new yeast cell all to itself. Before yeast cells can grow, they must have oxygen. The yeast plants in the jar are deep under the water, so they cannot get free oxygen from the air. In order to get oxygen, they manufacture a substance we call a ferment. This ferment breaks the sugar down into oxygen (which the yeast cells use) and a waste material, **carbon dioxide. Carbon dioxide** is a gas and, as it escapes from the water, it causes bubbles to rise to the top of the jar.

Another waste material, formed at the same time, is known as alcohol. It is a liquid and stays in the

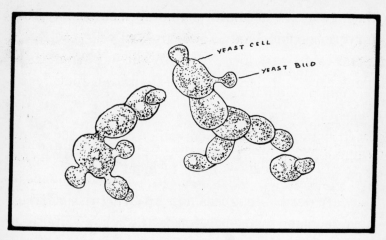

These are the growing yeast cells and their buds seen through the microscope, which enlarges them several hundred times their natural size.

water. When the sugar has all been used, the yeast cells stop growing, because there is no more food for them. If more sugar is added to the water, the yeast cells will begin to grow again. Finally, however, so much alcohol is formed that it will stop the yeast cells from growing even when sugar is present.

Until near the end of the Nineteenth Century, we knew very little more about what caused fermentation than did the people of ancient times. Then came Louis Pasteur, one of the greatest of all scientists. He discovered that fermentation is caused by the yeast cells. He found that if the yeast or plant cells could not get into the sugar water, there would be no fermentation. In addition to the yeast cells which produce alcohol, he found other plant cells, each with a different ferment to do a different job. When these plant cells were killed, no fermentation took place. We take advantage of Pasteur's discovery in the process of canning and preserving. When food is sealed in cans and boiled, the cells are killed and the contents of the cans will not ferment or spoil.

The yeast in dough causes bread to rise. Carbon dioxide gas is formed just as in the sugar water, but the gas bubbles are trapped or caught in the sticky dough and cannot escape. The gas bubbles cause the dough to swell and this makes the bread light. The old-fashioned name for loaf bread is lightbread.

Distillation.—Alcohol is formed in sugar water and is mixed with the water. When between ten and fifteen per cent of the water is replaced by alcohol, fermentation stops and no more alcohol is formed. Now the alcohol must be removed from the water before it can be used. The way in which alcohol is removed from water is very interesting. Let us find out how this is done.

You have seen a kettle of water boiling merrily on the stove. As the water boils, the steam rises and, finally, all the water will be gone. We say the water

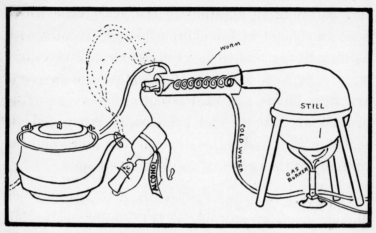

The still is used to separate alcohol from water. When steam comes off from the kettle, it is taken up by the air.

has boiled away. If you put a centigrade or chemical thermometer in boiling water the mercury will rise to the 100 degree mark (212 degrees on the Fahrenheit or weather thermometer), because that is how hot water gets when it boils. Alcohol boils at 80 degrees centigrade (176 degrees Fahrenheit) and the alcohol steam will come off at this temperature. This means that the alcohol in the water will boil and turn to steam first, and if the temperature is kept at 80 degrees, the water will never boil. If the alcohol steam escapes into the room, it will be taken up by the air since the air can hold a great deal of moisture.

In order to separate the alcohol from the water, we must make use of a special outfit called a **still.** A still, as you can see from the picture, is nothing more than a big boiler with a hollow coiled tube coming over from the top of the lid. When the alcohol steam begins to form, it passes down the coiled tube, which is called the worm. The lower end of the worm is enclosed in a jacket through which cold water is allowed to run continuously. The water in the jacket cools the outside of the worm but does not get to the alcohol. When the alcohol steam reaches the cool part of the worm, it condenses and changes back to its liquid form. This liquid is the alcohol which is now free from most of the water. The alcohol runs out at the end of the worm and is collected in vessels set to catch it. This process is called distillation and is used in the chemistry laboratory to separate not only alcohol from water, but also for many other chemical substances which have different boiling temperatures.

HOW ALCOHOL IS USED

The manufacture of alcohol is a big industry. Between two and three hundred million gallons of pure alcohol are made in the United States each year. This amounts to more than two gallons for each man, woman, and child in the whole country. Of course, when we hear someone talking about alcohol, we usually think of it in the form of whiskey, wine, beer, or some other alcoholic drink. Many millions of gallons of alcoholic beverages or drinks are sold each year. Beverage alcohol is made by special manufacturing methods, which are somewhat different from the methods used in making pure alcohol.

The chemical name of pure alcohol is ethyl alcohol. Most of it is made from sugar, molasses, and grain. Ethyl alcohol is important in a great many industries. It is used in the manufacture of hundreds of things we use every day. Almost anything that will dissolve in water can also be dissolved in alcohol. A great many substances which cannot be dissolved in water will dissolve quite easily in alcohol. This makes alcohol a very useful and valuable chemical. Alcohol is so important in industry that scientists have classed it as one of the six most important organic substances. Much of our progress in industry during the past twenty-five years would have been slowed up without alcohol. Many industries depend entirely on alcohol for their existence.

In the chemistry laboratory alcohol is next to water in importance. Without it, many chemical processes would become difficult, or even impossible.

Have you ever been in the zoology museum where dead specimens of animals or insects are preserved in glass jars? The fluid in these jars is usually alcohol. Small animals, fish, and snakes can be put in glass jars filled with alcohol and long years later will look almost like living animals. The alcohol enters the muscles of the specimen to kill the bacteria. The alcohol remains in the specimen to keep it from shrinking. This gives it the same appearance it had when alive.

Many years ago the Indians preserved their venison or deer meat by drying it in the sun. The dried meat would remain sweet for a long time. The bacteria which caused meat to spoil were without water and could not grow. When the fresh steak you buy is left out of the ice box, the bacteria will grow in it and cause it to spoil. You will remember, too, that yeast cells cannot grow without water. The museum specimen could be dried as the venison was, but it would then not look as it did when it was alive.

Perhaps some of you have had an operation and were put to sleep. If not, you know someone who has had such an experience. The substance used to put people to sleep is called an anesthetic (ăn′-ĕs-thĕt′-ĭc). The best and most commonly used anesthetic is ether. It is used because it is so safe that when properly given, it cannot cause death. Ether is made from alcohol, so that without alcohol, there would be no ether. In this way, alcohol helps to save many lives. Over two million gallons of alcohol are used each year

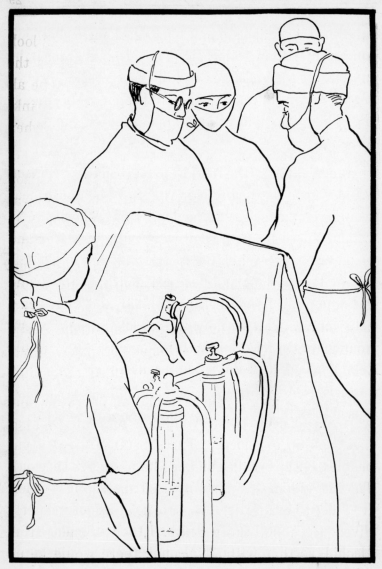

This is the picture of surgeons doing an operation on a sick person.
Alcohol was used to make the ether, kill germs on the patient's skin,
on the surgeon's hands, and on the surgeon's instruments.

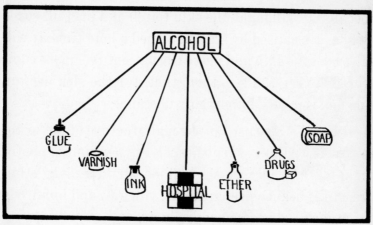

Alcohol has a great many uses.

in the manufacture of ether. Other drugs, almost as important for our sick people as ether, require the use of alcohol in their preparation. Some drugs made from plants, roots, and seeds must be made up in alcohol so that they will keep their full strength. If water is used, the drugs soon mold and spoil. Alcohol is used in making over four thousand different kinds of medicine.

In the hospital alcohol is perhaps one of the most important substances used. From it is manufactured ether and many drugs, as we have just learned. In addition, it is used to sterilize or cleanse the patient's skin because it is a germicide; that is, it kills germs. Catgut, which is used for sewing up wounds, is preserved in alcohol. Patients are rubbed with alcohol because it will make the skin tough and prevent sores which are caused by staying in bed a long time. It will also cool the skin and make the patient feel more comfortable. We can see, then, that, for the sick person, alcohol is a very important substance.

Alcohol is also used in the manufacture of flavoring extracts, paints, varnishes, dyes, perfumes, photographic and picture-show films, dry ice, ink, ethyl gasoline, beauty preparations, vinegar, and hundreds of other very necessary products.

From the time you get up in the morning until you go to bed at night, scarcely a minute passes when you are not using something which alcohol helped to make. The soap you use in the morning, your tooth paste, the handle on your hair brush, the mirror before which you comb your hair, the buttons on your coat, the dye in your clothing, all were made with the aid of alcohol. The varnish on the floor and furniture, the finish on your desk tops, the books you study and the glue that holds the pages together—alcohol helped to make them all.

No wonder alcohol is so important, and no wonder so much of it is made! There is every good reason to believe that, at some time in the future, when our natural supply of coal and gasoline has been used up, we will run automobiles and heat homes with alcohol.

REVIEW

1. Six thousand years ago the Egyptians began to record, in carved stone, the earliest stories of civilization.

2. Alcoholic beverages or drinks were first mentioned in some of the carved picture stories of the Egyptians about 5,000 years ago.

3. In Biblical history the use of fermented drinks was well known. Wine making was a flourishing industry.

4. The making of fermented alcoholic drinks probably began by accident with the very dawn of civilization.

5. Pure alcohol is a liquid which looks very much like water. Simple tests show, however, that there is a big difference between alcohol and water.

6. Alcohol is made by a process called fermentation. This process is caused by yeast cells which break sugar down and leave a waste product in the form of alcohol.

7. Alcohol is removed from the water, in which it is formed, by a process called distillation. The separation of alcohol from water is made possible by the difference in the temperatures at which they boil.

8. The name of pure alcohol is ethyl alcohol. Hundreds of millions of gallons of ethyl alcohol are manufactured in the United States each year. It is one of our most valuable chemical substances. It is used:

   (a) In chemistry as a solvent.

   (b) In the manufacture of hundreds of necessary things we use daily.

(c) As a preservative for museum specimens, as well
as many other things.

(d) In the preparation and manufacture of medicines
and ether.

(e) In the hospital as a germicide, a preservative, and
for rubbing the skin of sick people.

QUESTIONS AND THOUGHT PROBLEMS

1. What is the substance in rice which, when properly
treated, will form alcoholic wine?

2. Who was Belshazzar?

3. Explain what is meant by fermentation.

4. Tell, in detail, how alcohol is removed from water.

5. See how many uses, not mentioned in the text, you can
find for pure alcohol.

Unit II.

OUR PROBLEM

----

1. Why We Learn About Alcohol.

2. Whiskey, Wine and Beer.

OUR PROBLEM

Sometimes our problem is one which concerns no one except ourselves. At other times it may be much bigger and wider, and concern not only ourselves, but the whole civilized world.

We are going to study a problem which does concern people everywhere and perhaps their future. In the past it has been a moral problem to be talked about only by the preacher. In our study we will learn something about this problem, but in a different and most interesting way.

WHY WE LEARN ABOUT ALCOHOL

By now you are beginning to wonder why we are learning about alcohol. Well, here is the main reason: Of course, pure ethyl alcohol is too strong to drink, but millions and millions of people all over the world do drink whiskey, wine, or beer because such preparations contain alcohol. People drink these for the effects which the alcohol has on the brain. Are the effects on the brain and body good or bad? The answer to this we shall attempt to find.

We have already learned what a useful substance pure ethyl alcohol is. We know that as far back as written history goes, alcohol has been used as a beverage or drink.

Some of you have seen people who were drunk or, as we say, under the influence of alcohol. The problem resulting from the use and influence of alcohol has become so important that we should begin to learn something about its effects on the human body. Step by step we shall try to learn the truth about what alcohol, either in large or small amounts, may do to those people who drink it. Much has been written about alcohol. Many careful studies have been made within the past thirty years to find out what it actually does to the body. These studies represent the work of scientists whose truthfulness and accuracy cannot be doubted. These scientists are neither for nor against alcohol. Their only interest is to find the truth.

Study and try to understand the facts that have been found. In such a study you should learn many interesting things, all of which can be worth a great deal to you in later life. The boys and girls of past years did not have an opportunity to learn such truths and, as a result, have grown up without a knowledge that is both interesting and useful—a knowledge which will be yours.

WHISKEY, WINE AND BEER

Whiskey is made by fermenting ground corn, rye, or other grains. These grains contain a great deal of starch, which is easily changed into sugar. From this sugar, the yeast forms alcohol just as it did in the sugar water. When the grain mixture is distilled, other substances are carried over through the worm of the still with the alcohol to give it a flavor. It is now whiskey. It was not until about seven hundred years ago that the process of distillation was used in making whiskey. This process had its European beginning in Scotland and Ireland. The distilleries of these two countries today produce about 4,000 brands of whiskey.

A moonshiner's still used for making whiskey.

Wine is made by pressing the juice from grapes or certain other fruits. Sugar is added to the juice, and the jars filled with this juice, are left in a warm place. It is not necessary to put yeast in the juice because wild yeast cells get into it from the air and from the grape hulls. Alcohol is formed in the same way that it was formed in the sugar water, and finally the juice becomes wine. It is used in this form, since wine is not a distilled drink. If no sugar is put into the juice, it will still make wine, because of the grape sugar present in the grapes. Sugar is added to the juice to increase the amount of alcohol in the wine.

When fresh grape juice is boiled, the yeast cells are killed. If the boiled juice is sealed in bottles, it will not make wine, but becomes the grape juice which is served in the drug store. This kind of grape juice does not contain alcohol.

Beer is made from sprouted grain. It is fermented by a special kind of yeast cell which is different from the yeast used in making wine. By adding malt to the mixture, a process known as malting takes place. This gives alcoholic beer with a flavor different from wine or whiskey. Malt is made from grain, usually barley, which is dampened and allowed to sprout. It is then dried and is known as malt.

All of these contain alcohol.

In our study, we shall use the word alcohol instead of the names whiskey, brandy, rum, wine, ale, or beer. All of these are alcoholic drinks. We are interested only in the effects of alcohol, regardless of the form in which it is used. The alcoholic beverages are used instead of pure alcohol because all of them are flavored by substances to give a more pleasant taste. We have learned that pure ethyl alcohol is not used as a drink, because it is very strong and burns the throat.

REVIEW

1. We learn about alcohol because it is the substance in whiskey, wine, and beer which produces intoxication or drunkenness.

2. In our study we are interested mainly in the effects alcohol may have on the human body. If alcohol affects the body, wouldn't you like to know what that effect is?

3. Ours will be a study of science and what scientists have found in their laboratories.

4. Whiskey is made by fermenting grain in water. The alcohol, with the grain flavor, is then removed from the water by the process of distillation.

5. Wine is made from fruit juices which are allowed to ferment, but are not distilled.

6. Beer is made from sprouted grain by a special malting process. It does not taste like either whiskey or wine.

QUESTIONS AND THOUGHT PROBLEMS

1. Why should you know about the effects of alcohol on the human body?

2. What is the difference between the amounts of alcohol in whiskey, wine and beer?

3. What effect does boiling have on fresh grape juice?

Unit III.

ALCOHOL IN THE TREATMENT OF DISEASE

---

1. The Age of Science.

2. Old-Fashioned Remedies.

3. The Doctor and Alcohol.

4. Patent Medicines.

ALCOHOL IN THE TREATMENT
OF DISEASE

Science—what a simple word and yet how much it
has meant to man! It has led him from darkness to
light, from hardship to more leisure, from ignorance
to knowledge and power, and from superstition to
truth. Science is the one word that touches every
man's welfare and happiness. The science we are interested in here is that of medicine. In the dark ages
at times so many people died from disease that they
lay in the houses and streets with no one to bury them.
Now things like that could not happen, because medical science has learned not only how to treat but how
to prevent disease. Would you like to know something
about how medical science learns things which help
sick people to get well? In the section which follows
you will see how we have almost stopped using alcohol
as a medicine in that respect because it has little value.

THE AGE OF SCIENCE

Within a period of fifty years, doctors have learned more about the treatment of diseases than had been known for hundreds of years before. This fifty-year period has been called the golden age of scientific medicine. True science does not guess; it learns new things by carefully controlled experiments or studies. In these experiments, science finds out not only what happens, but how and why the things happen. Such studies have made the world a much safer and better place in which to live.

Scientists are the men whose dreams and hopes have been always to make people healthier and happier. Through the years their tireless efforts have conquered many dread diseases. Smallpox, yellow fever, cholera—names which once made the civilized world tremble with fear—are now little more than unpleasant memories on the pages of medical history. While men have waged war against each other, science has been at war with disease. The immortal Louis Pasteur, at the opening of the Pasteur Institute in 1888, said:

"Two opposing laws seem to me now in contest. The one, a law of blood and death, opening out each day new modes of destruction, forces na-

The laboratory is the workshop of the scientist.

tions to be always ready for the battle. The other, a law of peace, work and health, whose only aim is to deliver man from the calamities which beset him. The one seeks violent conquests, the other the relief of mankind. The one places a single life above all victories, the other sacrifices hundreds of thousands of lives to the ambition of a single individual. The law of which we are the instruments strives even through the carnage to cure the wounds due to the law of war. Treatment by our antiseptic methods may preserve the lives of thousands of soldiers. Which of these two laws will prevail, God only knows. But of this we may be sure, that science, in obeying the law of humanity, will always labor to enlarge the frontiers of life."

OLD-FASHIONED REMEDIES

Less than one hundred years ago the treatment of disease was largely guesswork and old-fashioned home remedies. The mad dog's bite was treated by the magic madstone, taken from the gall bladder of a deer. Wounds were filled with black soot from the chimney. Roots and herbs were gathered from the woods to be used for many an ache and pain. Alcohol, in the form of whiskey, stood on the front shelf of every medicine cabinet. No pain was too bad; no fever too high for alcohol to conquer.

If a person fainted, his jaws were pried open and in went some alcohol. The alcohol would stimulate him. Did it? Our studies of the past few years tell us alcohol depresses or weakens the functions of the body. On fainting the person was already depressed; his blood pressure was low, and very little blood was carried to the brain. So the alcohol did not help. Its use was dangerous. By breathing the strong alcohol odor, the person might gasp and become conscious. Smelling of strong ammonia would do the same thing and not be dangerous to life.

The poison from snake bite and alcohol once went hand in hand. People could not think of the bite without its cure—alcohol. Science taught us what we did not know, that poison from the snake's teeth affects the body by causing the blood pressure to fall. When this happens, the vessels that carry the blood to all parts of the body are not well filled and the heart is not able to pump blood where it should go. It was thought that the alcohol would kill the poison. Often the bitten person was given as much as a pint of whiskey. This amount of alcohol, added to the effect of the snake's poison, was perhaps enough to kill him.

Heatstroke is a condition caused by working in the sun and getting too hot. The person affected becomes very weak, and usually faints. In some way the heat causes blood pressure to become low and very little blood is carried to the brain. In the days of our grandfathers, alcohol was again the medicine for heatstroke. Now we know alcohol will only add trouble to what heatstroke has already brought. More than that, we know that people who have been drinking alcohol in large amounts, will have heatstroke more easily than when they have not been drinking.

At one time it was common belief that alcohol by its regular use would make the body strong and robust. At the same time, it was thought that the use of alcohol would protect one against infection. For this reason, it was taken to prevent colds and pneumonia, as well as many other diseases. Both ideas were not only foolish, but they were dangerous as well. Later on we shall see that alcohol breaks down the natural defenses of the body against disease and gives the germs a weakened navy of white blood cells to fight.

A few years ago if a person became thin and fell below his regular weight, he was advised to drink beer. Many people still drink beer because it increases body fat. Beer drinkers do get fat. The kind of fat put on by beer drinkers has been the subject of much study. Beer fat is a soft, shapeless fat. In certain European countries both men and women drink enormous quantities of beer. As a result, they become fat and shapeless and are, of course, very unattractive. The young girls who drink beer do not stay slender very long. They become fat and lose their shape as the older women do. Such large amounts of beer finally cause a condition known as beer heart. The heart becomes much larger than it should be and is fatty. In the muscles of a normal heart there is no fat. A fatty heart is weak, and this may finally result in the death of the person having it many years before the end of his or her natural lifetime.

THE DOCTOR AND ALCOHOL

Not many years ago doctors used a great deal of alcohol in the treatment of sick people. Very little was known then about the real effects of alcohol on the human body. This was before the day of scientific medicine. The alcohol was given as a stimulant and as a food. It is now a well-known fact that alcohol is not a true food, although it can sometimes be used in sickness for this purpose.

One of the diseases treated by the use of alcohol was pneumonia. Pneumonia is a very serious disease

The old-fashioned doctor thought alcohol was good for many diseases.

and kills about twenty-five out of every hundred people who have it. Pneumonia patients have severe pains in their chests and breathing is difficult because of the pain and inflammation. When the patients are given alcohol, they are more comfortable and rest better. Their breathing is less painful and less difficult. This led the doctors to believe that alcohol could kill off the pneumonia germs in the body. What actually happened was that the alcohol depressed the brain so that the person did not feel the pain and he was then able to rest and sleep.

Later on in the age of science, medical men began to doubt the value of alcohol as it was given, in the treatment of pneumonia. Careful studies were made in an effort to find out the truth. Large groups of

pneumonia patients were treated with alcohol; other
groups with the disease were not given alcohol. From
studies of these groups came some valuable information. It was found that a great many more of the
patients out of every hundred died in the groups
treated with alcohol than died in the groups which
had no alcohol.

At one time it was a common practice to use alcohol
in the treatment of typhoid fever. It is seldom used
in that disease any more. It may be of some value in
a few cases where the patient is too weak to take food,
or when his stomach and intestines cannot digest the
food he has taken. Alcohol in very small amounts can
be absorbed into the body through the stomach and
intestines to furnish an easy supply of energy. It
furnishes this energy easily because it can be used
without being changed. Alcohol is taken directly into
the blood from the stomach and intestines and used
in this form by the body. When used in typhoid fever,
alcohol should be given in very small doses. In the old
days it was given in amounts much too large and was
probably harmful. We know that most people with
typhoid will get along better without alcohol.

Not many years ago tuberculosis was treated with
"rock and rye." This was a preparation of rock candy
dissolved in alcohol. It was harmful because the more

"rock and rye" the patient took, the better he felt and the more he moved around. Now tuberculosis is treated by keeping the patients in bed all the time so that they will use the least amount of energy possible.

We have come slowly from the time when doctors used a great deal of alcohol in the treatment of many diseases to the present when alcohol is used very little in the treatment of sick people. As we learn new things, many old beliefs must be given up or they must be changed. Some doctors still give small doses of alcohol to pneumonia patients. Its only value here is to help the sick person to get more rest and sleep. When used in this way it may be helpful, though many doctors do not agree with this view. For the same reason, alcohol is sometimes given to people who are old and feeble. These old people cannot work and they have nothing to do except to think about themselves and worry about what is to become of them. Finally, they cannot eat and sleep well. Small doses of alcohol may quiet their fears or worries and in that way give them better appetites and more sleep. If alcohol can give such old people the peace and rest they have earned and cannot get by other means, then perhaps its use is justifiable. The same use in younger people would of course be dangerous, because of the ease with which the habit of using alcohol may be formed.

PATENT MEDICINES

One of the big industries of our day is the manufacture and sale of patent medicines. Every newspaper you read carries advertising about medicines that it is claimed will help almost any ills of the human body. Letters are secured from people who have used such medicines, telling about the wonderful cures obtained. A great many of these patent medicines contain from ten to twenty-five per cent alcohol. They are really nothing more than patent medicine cocktails, or drinks which contain alcohol. When taken into the body they have the effect that the same amount of whiskey or wine would have. The person using the medicine feels better because of the alcohol and not from any power the medicine may have to cure sickness. The cost of patent medicine in this country runs to several hundred million dollars each year and, of course, results in making the seller rich at the expense of the people who buy. Some of the largest fortunes in our country have been made from the sale of patent medicines. The use of such remedies is not only foolish, but may be dangerous as well.

In Germany and some of the other European countries, the sale of patent medicines is carefully controlled by law.

You should not use these when you are sick.

REVIEW

1. In the new age of scientific medicine, scientists learn, by careful studies in the laboratory, how to care for sick people and how to keep well people from getting sick.

2. Only a few years ago, much sickness was treated by old-fashioned remedies. Even doctors were not very well trained, and their methods for treating disease were often poor because they were not scientific.

3. In our day diseases are carefully studied. Remedies for the treatment of diseases are worked out in the laboratory by scientists so that we know what a remedy does and how it acts.

4. One of the common remedies of the past was alcohol. It was thought to be good for almost any sickness, but we now know this is wrong.

5. Doctors also used alcohol to treat many diseases. Now they seldom use alcohol, because scientists have proved that alcohol has little value except in a very few conditions.

6. Many people try to doctor themselves by the use of patent medicines. Do you think this is a very wise thing to do?

QUESTIONS AND THOUGHT PROBLEMS

1. Look up the meaning of the words science, and scientist.

2. Look up in the library some of the important scientific discoveries of Louis Pasteur.

3. How many reasons can you give for not using beer to increase the body weight of thin people?

4. Why was alcohol once very commonly used in the treatment of people sick with pneumonia?

5. See if you can find out the difference between drugs and patent medicine.

Unit IV.

FOOD AND ITS DIGESTION

57

FOOD AND ITS DIGESTION

As far back as people have lived in the world, the problem of finding food has been a most important one. Our ancestors lived on the flesh of animals, wild berries, and vegetables found in the fields. Probably there were no methods for preserving food. Later, when people began to build homes and to settle down in one place, they learned to grow vegetables and to tame some of the wild animals. Gradually as the time passed, these ancestors of ours became farmers, tradesmen, and herdsmen. With these changes early civilization began

Life for us is quite different from what it was in the early days. The study of food and diet has become a science. The newly born baby, the growing child, and the grown man, have diets fitted to their own particular needs. In spite of the attention paid to diet, man has many diseases of digestion. Some of these are due to poorly balanced diet, and others are due to injurious substances which people put into their stomachs. In this section you will learn how the stomach may be injured, and digestion ruined by one of these substances—alcohol.

These help to make the balanced diet.

FOOD AND THE BALANCED DIET

Most of us eat three meals each day. Do you know what happens to this food? Before we try to find the answer, let us see if we agree on what food is. No doubt you will say food is anything we eat. Food is anything you eat which gives energy for work and play and, at the same time, keeps up body weight. If what you eat is in any way harmful to the body, it cannot be called a food. Of course the best food may be harmful if you eat too much of it.

What do you eat when you go to the table at meal time? Certainly you do not try to live on just one kind of food, even though you may like it very much. If you did that, you would be in trouble very soon. On the table sometime during the day you will find bacon, cream, butter or vegetable oils as mayonnaise. From such foods come the fats which keep up the body weight. Bread, oatmeal, sugar, fruits, potatoes, and syrup are carbohydrate foods. The carbohydrates are called fuel foods because they are used by the body to furnish energy. A third kind of food, which we call proteins, comes from such things as fish, lean meat, eggs, whole milk, cheese, peas, and beans. The proteins are used by the body for building muscles and for repair. By properly mixing up the fats, carbohydrates and proteins at meal time you can have a balanced diet. Such a diet must also contain vitamins and certain minerals.* A balanced diet is one which takes care of all the needs of your body. By having such a diet, you will grow; you will have plenty of energy, and your muscles will be strong.

HOW FOOD IS DIGESTED AND ABSORBED

Now let us find out what happens to the food. In the mouth food is broken up by the teeth and, at the same time, mixed with saliva. The food then passes to the stomach, where it is churned around by muscles in

---

*A balanced diet cannot be made up entirely of fats, carbohydrates and proteins. In addition to these there must be present certain other important substances. They are the vitamins and the minerals. Vitamins in small amounts are found in such foods as green vegetables, yeast, milk, butter, eggs, grains, fruits, lean meat, and codfish as well as some other fish.

The most important minerals are calcium, iron and iodin. They are found in certain foods. Both children and adults must have vitamins and minerals. Their absence from the diet will cause disease and finally death.

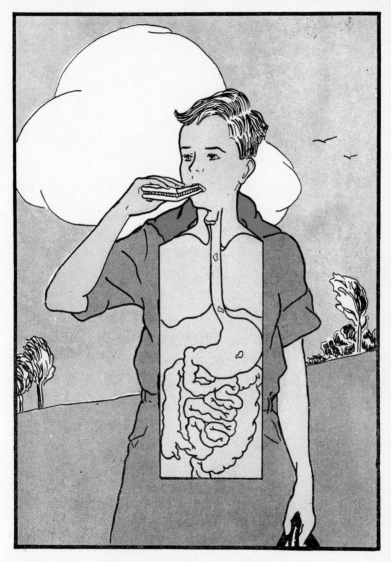

How food travels to the stomach.

the walls of the stomach until it looks very much like mush. While this churning process is going on, something else is happening. The inside of the stomach has a moist mucous lining and in this lining are many small glands. These glands pour out juices which help to break down carbohydrates, fats, and proteins so that the body can use them.

As soon as the stomach has finished its work, the mushy food material is shoved out into the small intestine. Here it is again squeezed and pushed around by the movements of the small intestine. In the mucous lining of the small intestine are found more glands, which also manufacture digestive juices. The juices from the stomach and small intestine soak out of the food everything the body can use. This dissolved food will now pass through the mucous lining of the small intestine into the blood vessels. From here it is carried all over the body to furnish materials for growth, energy, and repair.

In your own stomach the process of digestion goes on merrily. Each job is completed without a single worry or pain, for digestion is a very pleasant process. It is your good fortune to have a strong stomach with pink, healthy, mucous lining. Look at the inside of your mouth and you will see some mucous lining very much like the lining of the stomach. Notice the color and how soft and smooth it feels. Of course, the walls of the stomach and small intestine have in addition the tiny glands opening out on the mucous surface. Those glands are too small to be seen except through a microscope, but they certainly do a great deal of very important work.

The mouth, stomach, and intestines make up a very fine chemical laboratory. First the food is broken up, in the same way solid material in the laboratory is broken up, in order that the chemicals may get to it. In the stomach and intestines the chemicals are the digestive juices. Each one has a special job to do, but everything must be in exactly the right condition for it to work. In the laboratory we heat our test tubes over a gas flame and watch the chemicals in the tube bubble and boil. The chemical processes which take place in the stomach and intestines need only a small amount of heat. This is furnished by the heat of the body. As we shall see later, the body heat is controlled by a thermostat or heat control located in the brain. This thermostat gives exactly the right amount of heat for every chemical reaction in the body.

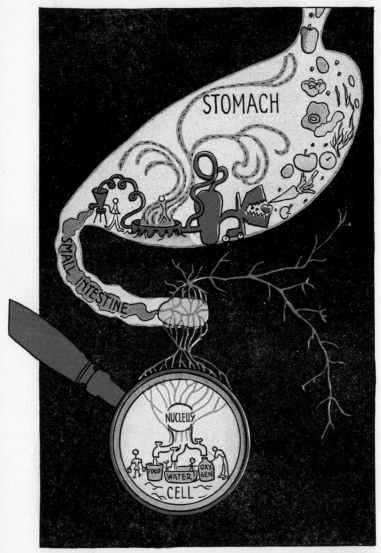

Food is broken down in the stomach and intestine. The queer looking machines seen in the picture were the author's boyhood idea of how the food is broken down and carried to the cells.

ALCOHOL AND THE STOMACH

Many things can happen to the stomach and intestines to keep them from doing good work. Sometimes people do not eat the proper kinds of food. Sometimes they put substances into their stomachs which do not belong there. One of the most common of these is alcohol.

When a person drinks alcohol his brain is numbed and he feels fine so long as this effect lasts. Later, when the effect has worn off, he feels much worse than before. Nearly everyone who gets drunk wakes up the next morning a very unhappy person indeed. There may be a severe headache and a feeling of nausea. If food is eaten, vomiting is the usual result. The mouth is dry and there is an unpleasant taste. Even large amounts of water do not satisfy the thirst. Alcohol takes water from the body, just as it takes water from the museum specimen.

If we were able to look inside the stomach of someone who is sick from the action of alcohol, we could understand why he is so upset. The delicate mucous lining of the stomach would be red and inflamed. Here and there might be seen tiny blood spots. Strong alcohol in the stomach burns the mucous lining and makes it very sensitive. When food gets to this stomach, the mucous lining is already so badly irritated or hurt that the food is sent right back out by a process we call vomiting. The glands that pour out digestive juices are upset, too, and do their work poorly or not at all. If this happens, the normal chemical reactions or changes are slowed up and any food left in the stomach sours.

We cannot look into the human stomach but we are able to do something that will tell us almost as much. We can fill the stomach of a small animal with alcohol. When this stomach is opened for examination, the usual pink mucous lining will be red and inflamed. The alcohol has injured the mucous lining. When a raw egg is broken into a dish of alcohol, the egg white has a cooked appearance, and it is cooked. Alcohol will do the same thing to some of the foods in the stomach.

What finally happens to the stomach of the man who has been drinking large amounts of alcohol for several years? His stomach looks much worse than the ones we have just talked about. The mucous lining, once delicate and pink, is not delicate and pink any longer. It is thick and has a leather-like appearance. The glands are not able to pour out nearly so much digestive juice as they should. They have been injured by the long continued use of alcohol. Some of the glands may be so badly injured that they have stopped working altogether. We would not expect the process of digestion in this stomach to be a pleasant one. The person with such a stomach has indigestion or stomach trouble a great deal of the time. He seldom feels well and he is never very happy.

REVIEW

1.   Food is anything we eat which provides for growth and energy, and at the same time does not injure the body.

2.   The food we eat should be in the form of a balanced diet. By this is meant we must have enough carbohydrates, fats, and proteins. As you will learn later, certain other things are necessary to complete the balanced diet.

3.   Food is broken up in the mouth. It then goes to the stomach where it is churned and mixed. It is acted on by the digestive juices of the stomach at the same time.

4.   The half-digested food passes to the small intestine. Here more digestive juices are poured out by the tiny glands. Finally, when digestion is completed, the food material in solution is soaked up by the delicate mucous membrane of the intestine. From here it passes into the blood to be carried to all parts of the body.

5.   When the mucous lining of the stomach and intestine is in good health, the glands pour out their juices properly and digestion goes on as it should go.

6. If alcohol is taken into the stomach, the delicate mucous lining is injured and the process of digestion is disturbed. Often food is vomited from such a stomach almost as soon as it is taken in.

7. By pouring alcohol into the stomach of a rabbit or other small animal, we are able to see the effects of the alcohol on the delicate mucous lining.

8. The stomachs of people who have been drinking alcohol for a long time, have a thick mucous lining. Digestion in such stomachs is never complete or pleasant.

QUESTIONS AND THOUGHT PROBLEMS

1. Can you name the things which go to make up a balanced diet? Make a list of these and tell why each one is necessary.

2. What must happen to food before the cells of the body can use it?

3. Compare the work of the mouth, stomach and intestine to the work done in the chemistry laboratory.

4. How does alcohol affect the process of digestion? Make a list of other things that can affect the digestion of food.

Unit V.

THE BODY BUILT OF LIVING CELLS

———

1. How Food is Prepared for the Cells.

2. The Organs Made of Cells.

3. Effects of Alcohol on Cells and Organs.

THE BODY BUILT OF LIVING CELLS

In 1675 Anton van Leeuwenhoek (Lēē'-wĕn-hŏk), a Dutch lens grinder, made the first microscope. With this microscope, he was the first man to see living cells. He did not know what they were and never did learn about their importance. More than 150 years later, a scientist named Schleiden showed that the body is made of cells.

We are going to study about the cells of the body and learn how very important they are. When seen through a microscope, the cells have the appearance of bricks laid together with cement. There are many different kinds of cells in the body and each kind has a different type of work to carry on.

HOW FOOD IS PREPARED FOR THE CELLS

You have learned how food is broken down and dissolved by the chemicals in the laboratories of the stomach and small intestine. We shall now look in on other busy laboratories of the body to find out where the food material is used. The mucous lining of the small intestine acts very much as an ink blotter—the dissolved food soaks through it. Fine networks of tiny blood vessels are located just under the thin layer of mucous lining. Most of the food passes through the thin walls of these vessels and goes into the blood. The fat from the intestine goes into the blood, too, but it takes a different route.

Blood, with its load of food, is collected in one big vein and carried into a large organ called the liver. The liver is a storehouse, as well as a preparation laboratory. Some of the food not needed by the body is stored in the liver, to be used between meals or when we are working hard and need extra food. The liver also takes waste materials out of the food which sometimes get through the walls of the small intestine and stomach. After the liver has finished its work, the food passes on out into another big vein which takes it to the pumping station (the heart). From here it is carried to every part of the body.

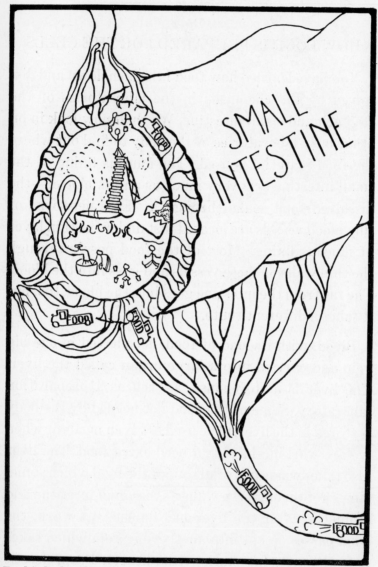

Food is broken down by the digestive juices and passes from the small intestine into the blood, to be carried to the cells of the body.

Our bodies are made up of billions of tiny units called cells. These cells are grown together so that they cannot move from their stations. Each cell has its own existence, just as each of us has ours. Cells breathe, take in food, do work, and send out wastes. Cells do not think, of course, but they do some very intelligent things. We think for the cells and we help them by careful living and good habits. If we take injurious substances into our bodies, the cells are disturbed and some of them may die. When we are sick, what has actually happened is that the cells are sick. In many diseases poisons are formed by germs growing in the body. These poisons go to the cells and soon the cells are unable to do their work properly. If enough cells are overcome by the poisons, the sick person dies. When we are in good health, each cell gets its food, its water, and as we shall see later, its oxygen to turn food into energy and work.

THE ORGANS MADE OF CELLS

The cells are the living stones in the building we call the human body. These cells are grouped into laboratories and each laboratory is a busy place so long as we live. Cell laboratories are called organs, and each organ is made up of special cells which do one kind of work. Even in one organ there will be found

groups of cells, each doing its own special work. In
the brain, for instance, are located cells for thinking,
as well as cells which do other things. The cells of the
stomach and intestine prepare food for all the other
cells. The cells of the liver act as a storehouse and a
station for destroying poisons. The cells of the kidney
form urine and get rid of body wastes. The cells of
the brain could never be made to form urine, and the
kidney cells would never learn to think.

EFFECTS OF ALCOHOL ON CELLS AND ORGANS

What does this have to do with the effects of alcohol
on the body? Alcohol upsets the life of all the cells, and
while it may not kill these cells, it certainly does injure them. We saw how the mucous lining of the
stomach is injured and thickened by alcohol. Now, the
same blood that carries food away from the stomach
also carries away certain waste materials formed
there. In ordinary amounts, the liver destroys these
wastes or poisons. When the lining membrane of the
stomach has been injured and thickened by alcohol,
some of the digestive juices are no longer poured out.
This results in the formation of larger amounts of
waste materials which injure living cells. The liver
is not able to destroy the increased amounts of poison

coming to it. When this happens, the liver cells become swollen and injured. Then the liver is not able to do its very important work in the way it should be done and all the cells of the body suffer, because of the poisons which get to them. Experiments show that a liver damaged by the use of alcohol is injured by other poisons which have no effect on the normal liver.

Alcohol is taken into the blood through the mucous lining of the stomach and small intestine. Not a great deal of alcohol can be found in the blood at any one time, but there may be present amounts which are large enough to interfere with the life of the cells. Many people are made sick by the use of alcohol. This sickness is due to the effect of alcohol on the cells.

Alcohol, as you have already learned, is a germicide or germ killer and, as such, has the power to kill germs. In this strength it will also kill cells. Fortunately, when people drink alcohol, it is not found in the cells in large amounts. These amounts are so small that we have no laboratory tests delicate enough to measure the effects on the cells. Five parts of alcohol in one thousand parts of blood may be enough to cause death. It is reasonable to think that if such a small amount of alcohol in the blood can kill a person, then smaller amounts will injure cells. Later we shall study the life insurance records and see that people who drink alcohol do not live as long as those who do not drink it.

REVIEW

1.   Food passes through the mucous lining of the small intestine into the blood.

2.   After food gets into the blood it is carried to the liver. Here it is purified and some of it is stored. The food which is not stored begins its journey to the cells.

3.   The body is made up of billions of tiny cells. They must have food, water, and oxygen brought to them.

4.   The cells are grouped into organs. The work going on in the body all the time is divided up among the organs. Each organ does its own special work. The brain thinks; the stomach and intestine prepare food; the liver purifies food and acts as a storehouse; the kidneys get rid of body wastes: the lungs take in oxygen and give off carbon dioxide.

5.   Alcohol disturbs the life of cells and organs. It injures the stomach and causes poisons to increase. It injures the liver and keeps it from purifying the food which goes to the cells.

6.   Five parts of alcohol in one thousand parts of blood may cause death.

QUESTIONS AND THOUGHT PROBLEMS

1.   Can you name the different kinds of work done by the liver?

2.   What are cells and how do they live?

3.   What are organs?

4.   How does alcohol affect the cells of the body?

Unit VI

THE CIRCULATION OF THE BLOOD

1. The Pipe Line to the Cells.

   A. The Heart.

   B. The Arteries.

2. How Alcohol Affects the Heart and Arteries.

THE CIRCULATION OF THE BLOOD

Three hundred years ago William Harvey, an English doctor, discovered how blood flows and how the heart pumps the blood. Many people thought Harvey was crazy, and only a few of his friends believed him. Now all of us know that blood from a cut finger comes from the veins, and that the pulse is caused by the heart pumping blood to all parts of the body.

The Egyptians of ancient times believed the mind was located in the heart. To all ancient peoples the heart was the center for love. Even now we use the expression "I love you with all my heart." It is natural that people should feel this way, because the heart is a remarkable organ. It beats without stopping from the time life begins until the last moment of life. The only rest the heart gets is about a half second between beats, but that is enough. Most people expect their hearts to do good work but they will not do anything to make that work easier. They eat too much, get too fat, take no exercise, stay up late, and drink alcoholic beverages. Finally many of them die from heart disease.

THE PIPE LINE TO THE CELLS

We have learned that the cells of the body do work. Wherever work is done, energy or power is used. This energy must be produced from raw material in the form of dissolved food. When energy is produced, waste materials are formed. This means that the cells must have food brought to them and waste products removed; just as coal is carried to the furnace and ashes are taken away. Every cell in the body has a pipe line running directly to it to carry food and take away wastes. We shall now study and try to understand this interesting pipe line to the cells. Like most of the machinery of our body, we know that it is there, but few of us take the time to learn about it. The human body is a remarkable machine, and you will do well to learn all you can about it.

The Heart.—The circulatory system, or the pipe line, as we shall call it, is made up of the heart, or pump; the arteries, which are the lines from the heart to the cells; and the veins, which are the lines from the cells back to the heart. In the picture you can see that the heart is divided into four sections. These sections are like chambers or rooms. They are separated from each other by valves or gates which allow the blood to go only in one direction. The upper two cham-

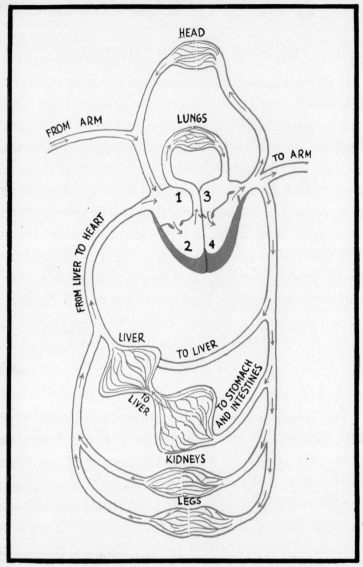

HEAD

FROM ARM

LUNGS

TO ARM

FROM LIVER TO HEART

1   3

2   4

LIVER

TO LIVER

TO LIVER

TO STOMACH AND INTESTINES

KIDNEYS

LEGS

*The heart pumps the blood to all parts of the body with its load of food,
water, and oxygen. In the picture the part in red represents the
blood on the way to the cells, and the blue represents
the blood returning from the cells.*

bers take the blood in and the lower two pump it out. Blood coming through the veins from all over the body is emptied into the first chamber. When the first chamber is filled, the little valve or gate is opened and the blood flows into the second chamber. The blood from this chamber is pumped through the lungs. When the blood comes out of the lungs, it goes into a third chamber. Finally, the blood from this chamber goes down into the fourth chamber. The last of the chambers, or the fourth chamber, pumps the blood out into a large artery, where it starts on its journey to the cells.

Before going further, let us find out why the blood passes through the lungs. When we take air into our lungs, it fills the many little air sacs which make up the lungs. These air sacs are very thin and they are surrounded by networks of tiny blood vessels. The air we breathe contains oxygen. This oxygen is taken through the walls of the air sacs and the blood vessels to enter the blood. At the same time some of the waste products from the cells, in the form of carbon dioxide, are forced out of the blood into the air sacs. This carbon dioxide is then breathed out into the air.

The blood we are following through the heart has just come from the stomach and intestine, where it was loaded with food. In the lungs we find this same blood receiving a load of oxygen. Here, perhaps, you will agree that the blood is able to do some very wonderful things.

The Arteries.—A moment ago we left the blood in the fourth chamber of the heart. Now we can return to this point and see where the blood goes and how it travels. The arteries which carry the blood are thin and elastic, somewhat like rubber tubes. As they get farther away from the heart, these arteries become smaller, breaking up into millions of branches. The branches spread out in all directions. They go to all the organs as well as the trunk, head, arms and legs. Finally, the tiny branches end up in the skin in networks so fine that if a pin is stuck into the skin it will hit many of them.

The heart, by its pump action, forces blood along the arteries. The force of the heart beat causes the elastic arteries to swell or increase in size. As the arteries come back to their usual size, between heart beats, their walls squeeze down on the blood to keep it moving forward. The valves of the heart will not allow blood to flow backward in the arteries. The blood which flows to the cells does a number of things. It takes food to the cells from the stomach and intestines. It carries oxygen from the lungs to change the food into energy and body weight. It takes water to

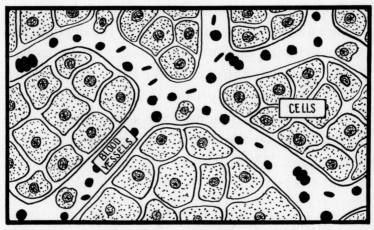

These are some of the cells of the body and the blood vessels that bring
them blood as seen under the microscope.

the cells to keep them moist and to help carry out the
chemical processes. When the blood leaves the cells,
it carries with it waste materials. Most of these waste
materials of the blood leave the body through the
kidneys, skin and lungs. Other body wastes escape
through the intestines.

HOW ALCOHOL AFFECTS THE
HEART AND ARTERIES

When alcohol is taken into the stomach, it finds its
way into the blood in the same way food does, and is
carried to the cells. The alcohol is, of course, dis-
tributed throughout the circulating blood. As you
have already learned, five parts of alcohol in 1,000

parts of blood may cause death. Usually there is not enough alcohol in the blood to cause the death of the person drinking it. For a long time everyone thought alcohol stimulated the heart. We know now that this is not true. Alcohol depresses the heart and makes it weak. After alcohol is used for a long time, it may cause a serious weakening of the muscles in the walls of the heart. These muscles become fat and flabby, so that the heart is not able to do its work properly.

It is claimed by some scientists that long continued use of alcohol causes the arteries to become less elastic, resulting in a condition which we call hardening of the arteries. No one has been able to prove this for sure and many scientists doubt the truth of it. We do know, however, that alcohol is not a good thing for the arteries, just as it is not a good thing for the rest of the body.

When a person is in good health there is enough blood in his arteries to keep them full. When the heart pumps more blood into a full artery, that artery gets a little fuller because it is like a thin rubber tube and can be stretched. The artery always tries to come back to its usual size. If alcohol is taken into the body, the small arteries are numbed and are no longer like rubber, with the result that they get large and flabby. Now there is not enough blood to fill the arteries, and the pressure in them becomes low. When the pressure in the arteries is low, the cells suffer because there is not enough blood going to them. This action of alcohol in dilating or making the small blood vessels (the capillaries) larger, comes from the effects of alcohol taken at any one time. The unproved belief that alcohol causes hardening of the arteries is based on its use over a long period of time.

If you water the lawn with a small hose, you can throw water a hundred feet or more. Now if you try to use a big hose four or five times as large, there will not be enough water to fill it and the water will barely run out through the nozzle. That is about what happens to the way blood flows when the arteries get too large.

REVIEW

1. Every cell in the body has a pipe line of blood vessels going to it to carry food, water and oxygen, and to bring away waste materials.

2. The pipe line is made up of the heart, which pumps the blood; the arteries, which carry blood to the cells; and the veins, which bring it away.

3. The blood coming from the stomach and intestines with its load of food is pumped through the lungs to get a load of oxygen.

4. Alcohol weakens the heart, and after continued use, injures it. Alcohol also causes the walls of the tiny arteries to weaken and become larger. When they get larger, there is not enough blood to fill them and the pressure of the blood becomes low.

QUESTIONS AND THOUGHT PROBLEMS

1. Tell how the heart is divided up, and how the blood is pumped through it.

2. What is the function of the blood?

3. In what possible ways may alcohol injure the heart and the arteries?

4. Trace the route of the food, carried by the blood, from the stomach to the cells.

Unit VII

THE TEMPERATURE OF THE BODY

---

1. How Body Temperature is Regulated.

2. Effect of Alcohol on Body Temperature.

THE TEMPERATURE OF THE BODY

In the next section the control of the body temperature is compared to a thermostat. This is a small electrical instrument located in the living room of homes and connected with the furnace to control the heat in winter. The thermostat has a special kind of metal in it which expands in a warm room and contracts in a cold room. When the metal contracts, it closes the electric switch and causes a fan to blow the fire. As the room gets warm the metal expands and cuts the electric current off to stop the fan. In this way the house is kept at the proper temperature in cold weather. The thermostat was invented only a few years ago.

Thermostats are, however, as old as life itself. All of us have thermostats in our brains. Of course, our brain thermostats do not look like furnace thermostats, and they work much better. Except in sickness the body temperature stays about the same all the time. In the next section you will learn something about how your bodies lose heat in summer and save it in the winter. You will also learn how the thermostat of the body can be thrown out of order even when there is no sickness.

HOW BODY TEMPERATURE IS REGULATED

The temperature of the body is controlled by a thermostat located in the brain. This thermostat, or regulator, keeps the temperature of the body from going up or down. In a healthy person, the body temperature always remains the same. The flow of the blood and the size of the blood vessels help regulate body heat. The tiny blood vessels in the skin are elastic as rubber. They can increase or decrease in size from time to time. In warm weather these tiny vessels become larger and more blood comes to the surface of the body. This blood is cooled by the air and sweat. The cool blood goes back into the body and more warm blood comes to the skin surface to take its place. This helps us lose the heat we do not need in summer weather. When you run and get hot, your body makes more heat than you need. In the process of getting rid of this extra heat, the skin gets red, because the small skin vessels are dilated and are full of blood. Then you sweat and cool this blood in your skin. In cold weather the body is not able to make more heat than it needs. It must now save all the heat possible. The little blood vessels in the skin contract, or close, so that very little warm blood goes to the outside. The warm blood stays deep in the body. When you are very chilly, you will have goose pimples on your skin. This means that the little blood vessels are almost completely closed so that the warm blood will stay deep in the body. By exercising you are able to help your body make more heat and you become warmer.

EFFECT OF ALCOHOL ON BODY TEMPERATURE

If the skin vessels are opened wide in cold weather, heat is lost faster than the body can manufacture it. When this happens, a person may freeze very quickly. For many years people took alcohol before going out into cold weather because it made them feel warm. In zero weather, the alcohol causes the skin vessels to open wide when they should be closed tight. The skin vessels are filled with warm blood and the skin feels warm. By the time the blood in the skin becomes cool, more warm blood comes to take its place and the cool blood is carried back into the body. Before long, however, there is no warm blood left, since the body is not able to heat it as fast as the air cools it. For this reason drunken people soon freeze if they are left out in extremely cold weather. Alcohol numbs the heat-regulating center in the brain and causes the blood vessels of the skin to dilate or open wide.

We can show by experiments in the laboratory how the use of alcohol in cold weather will cause the body to lose heat. A scientist gave one rabbit a small amount

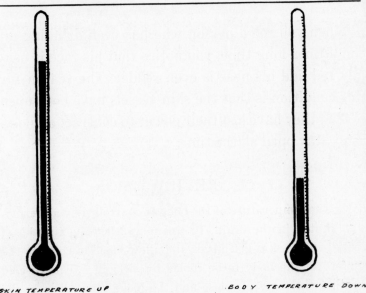

SKIN TEMPERATURE UP   BODY TEMPERATURE DOWN

Alcohol causes the temperature of the skin to rise but it causes the temperature of the deeper parts of the body to fall. For this reason drunken people freeze to death very quickly in zero weather.

of alcohol. He put this rabbit in an ice box at five degrees below zero by the Fahrenheit or weather thermometer. At the end of two and one-half hours the rabbit showed a fall of nineteen degrees in body temperature. Another rabbit with no alcohol was placed in the same ice box for the same length of time. The temperature of this rabbit fell a little more than three degrees. With alcohol there was a drop of nineteen degrees in body temperature; without alcohol there was a drop of three degrees. No wonder drunken people freeze easily. Since they become chilled quickly, drunken people also get colds and pneumonia more easily.

When you see a person who has been drinking alcohol for a long time, you notice that his face is usually red and his nose is even redder. The reason for this condition is that the skin vessels have been open so long they have lost their power to contract or close. They stay open all the time.

REVIEW

1.   The temperature of the body is controlled by a thermostat located in the brain. In warm weather the tiny blood vessels in the skin get larger and allow blood to come to the surface of the body to be cooled by air and sweat. In cold weather these vessels close and the blood stays deep in the body so that little heat will be lost.

2.   When alcohol is taken into the body, it causes the small blood vessels in the skin to become larger. These vessels are then filled with blood and the skin becomes red. In cold weather alcohol will cause a person to freeze to death because he loses heat when he should not.

3.   Experiments showed that rabbits which had been given alcohol and kept in a cold ice box, lost much more body heat than animals without alcohol in the same ice box.

QUESTIONS AND THOUGHT PROBLEMS

1.   How is the temperature of the body controlled?

2.   Explain how alcohol affects body temperature.

3.   Is alcohol a good substance to drink before going out into zero weather? How can you prove it is not?

Unit VIII

THE MASTER CONTROL OF THE BODY

———

1. The Brain and the Nerves.

2. How Alcohol Affects the Brain and Nerves.

3. Mental Diseases Caused by Alcohol.

THE MASTER CONTROL OF THE BODY

The human brain is one of the marvelous works of creation. Look around you and see the modern inventions, such as the telegraph, steam engine, radio, automobile and airplane. All of them are products of the brain of man. Nothing is half so remarkable as the power to think and to build thoughts into things that make life easier for all people.

In this section you can see how the brain looks, and learn something about how it works. The most important effect of alcohol on the body is seen in the brain.

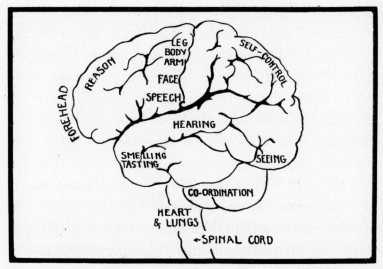

This is a picture of the human brain. It is the central office which receives messages from and sends messages to all parts of the body.

THE BRAIN AND NERVES

The brain is the master control of the human body. All animals have brains, but only one, man, has a very highly developed power to think. This places man at the head of the animal kingdom. Sometimes, perhaps, we have cause to wonder if that is where he belongs. The king of the animals should be perfect in every way; many times he is least perfect.

On this page is a drawing of the human brain. It is located in a bony box, called the skull. The skull is strongly built and protects the brain perfectly from a thousand accidents. In the brain are located places called centers, which give us the power to think. Other centers in it control seeing, hearing, feeling, tasting, smelling, talking, breathing, and walking. Every activity of the body from the simplest to the most difficult is under the control of the brain. Every part of the body is connected to the brain by means of nerves. There are thousands of these nerves and, as in the case with the tiny blood vessels, we cannot stick a needle into the skin without touching the endings of many nerves. The nerves are made up of glistening bundles of white fibres, and in their action, they remind us of telephone wires. The endings of the nerves out in the body are like telephones, for they pick up messages and send them to the brain. The brain is the central office which gets the right center or number and sends a message back in answer to the call. This message from the brain answers the question asked by the nerve ending, which is somewhere out in the body. An example of this telephone-like action takes place when you pick up a baseball in the dark. The nerve endings send a message to the brain, asking what has been picked up; what shape is it; how heavy, and how hard. The central office gets the proper center and back goes the answer: It is round; it is not heavy; it is hard; it is a baseball. By feeling you are able to recognize many things without the aid of sight.

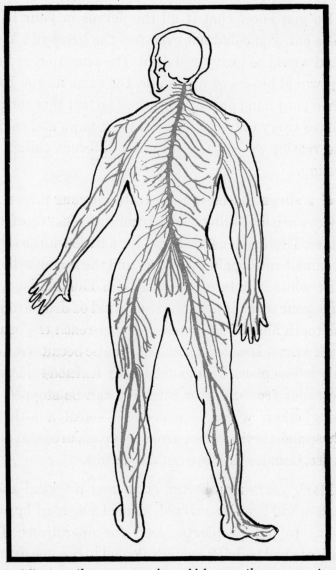

The red lines are the nerves or wires which carry the messages to and from the brain.

Do you know that if all the nerves in your hand were cut, you could not even feel the baseball? Your hand would be heavy and dead. The sensation or feeling would be one of numbness, the same as you have when your hand or foot is asleep. The fact that certain nerves carry only messages of heat, pain, and cold is the reason we can tell so many different things by feeling.

If a surgeon wishes to operate on your finger, he injects a pain-killing drug around the nerve of the finger. This deadens the nerve for a little while so that it cannot carry pain messages, and the finger will not hurt while it is being operated on. The dentist who pulls your tooth injects the same kind of drug around the tooth and no pain messages can reach the brain. Such a drug is called a local anesthetic because it acts only in one place. You have already learned that pain messages from all over the body can be stopped by using ether, which is called a general anesthetic. These anesthetics, when properly given, are good ones to use, because they are not dangerous.

Many years ago, before ether and the local anesthetics had been discovered, alcohol was used by surgeons to put people to sleep for operations. The patients had to drink enough alcohol to become drunk. In this condition, their bodies were numbed and they did not feel very much pain. Alcohol is a dangerous anesthetic. Patients often died from its effects back in the days when it was used as an anesthetic.

HOW ALCOHOL AFFECTS THE BRAIN AND NERVES

Alcohol has its first and most important action on the brain and nervous system. Here from beginning to end it is purely narcotic; that is it depresses. Narcotic pronounced (när-kŏt´ĭk) is a Greek word which means to numb, or produce deep sleep. Alcohol has this depressing or numbing action on all parts of the nervous system.

For many years people thought a little alcohol, that is, a few drinks, could have no bad effects on the brain. Then scientists worked out many delicate tests and, by their results were able to show that alcohol, even in small amounts, does have a very definite effect on the brain and nervous system. Later we shall learn about some of these tests and what they show.

People drink alcohol because of the peculiar effects it has on the brain. It gives them a feeling of comfort and careless lack of concern about what happens. It releases them, for the moment, from their worries, troubles, and pain. They are usually pleasant and talk a great deal. Often they become loud and boisterous.

Alcohol takes away the control which the thinking part of the brain has over the persons drinking it. Finally, they feel heavy and numb and fall into a deep sleep, lasting, perhaps, for many hours.

People who drink alcohol usually fall into three groups. The ones in the first group drink alcohol daily, but they do not become drunk. The people in the second group drink enough to become drunk, but they do not drink very often. In the third group are found the heavy drinkers who usually drink large amounts of alcohol every day.

People in the first group, the light drinkers, have long thought their drinking had no bad effects on the brain and body. Scientists, being interested in finding out the true effects of small amounts of alcohol on the brain, made some very interesting tests. These tests were made with people before and after they had been given small amounts of alcohol. The tests showed that after drinking even small amounts of alcohol, the people tested were slower and less accurate than before. Some of these people, who were trained typists, were asked to write on the typewriter, both before and after taking alcohol. After taking alcohol, they made many more mistakes and wrote much more slowly than they did before. Other people, who were tested, made more mistakes in doing arithmetic sums after taking alcohol. In every test the people actually thought they had done better after taking alcohol than before.

One group was tested on their ability to pay close attention. After taking alcohol, these people were not able to pay close attention. They were also not able to remember so well the things they heard as they were before.

In European countries wine and beer drinking is common, even among school children. Studies were made in the schools of these countries to see if there was any difference between the work of those children who drank wine and beer and those who did not. The children who did not drink wine and beer were usually the best students and led their classes. The children who used wine and beer were nearly always poor students and stood at the bottom of the classes.

A scientist, interested in the effects of alcohol on memorizing or learning, made some tests on himself. He memorized lines of poetry on days when he had no alcohol and lines on days when he had taken small amounts of alcohol. On the days when he took alcohol, he was not able to learn as many lines as he did on the days when he had taken no alcohol. He found that he forgot the lines learned on alcohol days much sooner than he did the lines learned on the other

days. One month after the experiment, he again studied the same lines which he had almost forgotten
and found it took much longer to relearn the lines
memorized on the alcohol days. This goes to show
that the mind does not learn as quickly, even with
small amounts of alcohol, and that it does not remember what it has learned as long.

We could go on telling about many experiments
which prove that small amounts of alcohol do have a
very harmful effect on the mind of the person who
drinks it. When you hear someone say that a little
alcohol does not affect the mind, you can tell him
about these tests. What he says is just what he thinks.
What you tell him is something you can prove.

For many years alcohol was called a stimulant. A
stimulant is a drug or medicine which increases the
activity of the body and mind. The idea that alcohol
had this kind of action came about because most
people show mild excitement after drinking it. As
we see them, such people have every appearance of being stimulated or excited. They talk a great deal,
they laugh, and they are more active. This so-called
stimulating effect of alcohol can be easily explained
by its action on the thinking part of the brain. We have
already said that man is king of the animals because
he can think and reason far better than the other

animals. The difference between the way people and animals act can be explained by differences in brain development. People have highly developed brain centers for thought and reason. These centers cause them to be modest, quiet, and thoughtful. They are courteous and kind to other people. Animals have no such highly developed brain centers and probably do very little real thinking. The best they can do is to learn a few things, and after a great deal of training, seem to understand some of the things you say to them. A dog barks very loudly and joyously even when someone in the house is so seriously sick that not a sound should be made. When people become intoxicated, or, as we usually say, drunk, their higher brain centers are depressed or numbed and they act like animals. Such people act like animals because only the animal or lower part of the brain is working. This explains why drunken people are loud and boisterous when they should be quiet. It explains why they often quarrel and fight, and even kill their best friends. The thinking or reasoning part of the brain is numbed to such an extent that it cannot control their actions. The animal part of the brain is in charge.

Certain centers in the brain and spinal cord are called the lower centers. Such centers control actions we do not have to think about. These actions are auto-

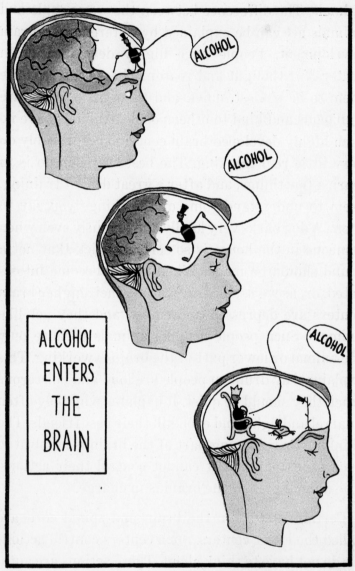

When alcohol enters the brain, it conquers reason and becomes king.

matic or involuntary, and are not under the control of the will. We breathe when we are asleep; even when we are awake we breathe without thinking about it. We walk along, thinking about other things besides walking, seeing, or hearing; yet, we walk, see, and hear more or less unconsciously. All of these actions take care of themselves. Animals breathe, walk, hear, and see in the same way but they do not think in the same way as we do. When enough alcohol is taken, even these lower centers are affected. A drunken man staggers and falls. He walks against the telephone pole. He cannot unlock the front door because he cannot find the keyhole. He does not hear well because his center for hearing is depressed. The reason these things happen is that the brain centers which control such actions are numbed or depressed by the alcohol. Finally, a large amount of alcohol may cause death, because the center for breathing is paralyzed or completely numbed and breathing stops.

MENTAL DISEASES CAUSED BY ALCOHOL

The drunken man today with the animal-like brain may be a sober man tomorrow with the brain of reason. When he is intoxicated, he is animal-like; when he is sober, he again becomes a man with sense and reason. But what of the man who continues to drink for years and years? To him many things may happen. The effects of alcohol are weakening and destructive to both mind and body. We often see very serious diseases caused by the use of large amounts of alcohol, taken over a period of years. Men differ in the way they are affected by alcohol at any one time, or even in a long time. In the end, however, the results are usually the same.

Mental Depression.—We see a man of neat appearance and bright mind who later becomes a heavy drinker. As time passes, we are able to see many changes. He becomes careless about his clothing; his suit is not pressed and his shoes are not shined. He does not get his hair cut often; he may go two or three days without shaving. Sometimes he goes to work late; sometimes he is too sick to go at all. He is not very kind and thoughtful to his family. At the office he neglects business and drives his customers or clients away by failing to do good work for them. He promises to do things but does not do them. Later he may become so changed that he is neither truthful nor honest. Finally he becomes depressed and sullen, with a weakening of the mind that can be noticed by everyone.

Some men, even though they use large amounts of alcohol, may be able to go on for years without stopping. One look at such men, however, tells us something is wrong. They are not mentally alert or alive. Their steps are slow and sluggish; their faces are usually red and always dull or lifeless. The flame of youth and enthusiasm is gone. The people who drink very much take no exercise. Sometimes they do not eat at all and at other times they eat large amounts of food. The body is always weakened and usually diseased. It is natural then that the mind also should become weakened.

That the long continued and heavy use of alcohol produces a loss of mental power and ability to think clearly, no one will deny. The signs of mental disease in such people is as plain as the signs of a cold. When these people quit drinking alcohol, so far as we can tell, they get well and are able to go on as they did before. We do not know how much injury remains in the cells, for medical science has not yet found ways to measure such injury. The human body has remarkable powers for repairing the injuries caused by disease. We doubt, however, that it can completely repair the injury caused by the long continued use of alcohol.

Delirium tremens (dĕ-lĭr′ĭ-ŭm trē′-mĕns).—This is a condition caused by the drinking of large amounts of alcohol. A common name given to it is the "horrors." A person with delirium tremens, or horrors, sees all sorts of horrible creatures, snakes, rats, spiders, and animals that never existed. He is surrounded by terrible goblins which make faces and grin at him. He screams in terror; he hides; he begs for someone to save him. He imagines bugs and mice are crawling under his skin and tries to tear them out. Usually, so much alcohol has been drunk that his stomach is injured and his digestive system is completely upset. This condition is brought on by a drunken spree, lack of food, failure to get more alcohol, or by some serious sickness following heavy drinking. A person with delirium tremens is usually very sick. He is completely exhausted; his whole body shakes as though he had a chill. He may get well after several days' treatment, or he may die.

Korsakoff's (Kôr-săk´-ŏf's) disease.—This is a very serious disease caused usually by the use of strong alcoholic beverages, such as whiskey and brandy. There are severe pains in the arms and legs due to diseased nerves. Usually, the person forgets what he has said. He may forget whether or not he has eaten a meal. He may not be able to recall what happened yesterday. He imagines queer things and makes up stories about events he thinks have actually happened.

People suffering from this disease very seldom get entirely well.

Alcoholic Hallucinosis (hăl-lū-sĭn-ō'-sĭs).—Alcoholic hallucinosis is another kind of mental disease, in which the person imagines he hears voices calling his name. He thinks people are watching him from hiding places, and that they wish to hurt him. Then, he becomes quieter and does not notice the voices, though he still thinks he hears them. Some of these people get well, but many of them do not.

Alcoholic Paranoia (păr'-à-no'ĭ-å).—Alcoholic paranoia is a serious mental disease in which the person may become suspicious of everyone around him. He is jealous of his wife and children. At times he may become violent and dangerous.

REVIEW

1. The brain controls nearly all activities of the human body. In the brain are located places called centers which control thinking, seeing, hearing, tasting, breathing, walking, talking, feeling and smelling.

2. Nerves run to and from the brain to all parts of the body. Messages go over these nerves to and from the brain. The brain and nerves act somewhat as a telephone system. The ends of the nerves are the telephones, the nerves are the wires and the brain is the central office.

3.   Alcohol depresses the brain and keeps it from receiving or sending messages properly. For this reason intoxicated people do not think, feel, see, hear, walk, or talk well. Only the lower or animal part of the brain is not depressed by ordinary amounts of alcohol.

4.   Tests show that even small amounts of alcohol disturb the ability to memorize, as well as the ability to carry on other mental activities.

5.   Alcohol was at one time used as an anesthetic for operations. It is not used for this purpose any more because it is dangerous. Safe anesthetics have been discovered to take the place of alcohol.

6.   People drink alcohol because it depresses the higher brain centers which control worry and pain. They feel good and do not think about their troubles.

7.   Even small amounts of alcohol cause people to make more mistakes in typing and in doing arithmetic sums. The ability to learn is also weakened.

8.   Alcohol causes a number of diseases of the mind. They vary from slight mental changes to complete insanity.

QUESTIONS AND THOUGHT PROBLEMS

1.   Make a list of the different kinds of work done by the brain.

2.   How does alcohol affect the working power of the brain?

3.   What is a stimulant? Why was alcohol once thought to be a stimulant?

4.   What are the lower brain centers?

5.   Tell how the lower centers of the brain are affected by alcohol.

Unit IX

INTENTIONAL OR VOLUNTARY MOVEMENTS

---

1. We Learn to Use Our Muscles.

2. Alcohol and the Muscles.

3. Alcohol and the Senses.

INTENTIONAL OR VOLUNTARY MOVEMENTS

Since the very beginning of civilization, man has lived by the use of his muscles and, of course, of his mind. Early man had to depend entirely on muscle power in his struggle to live. He probably climbed up on high cliffs to drop heavy stones on the skulls of animals he wanted to kill for food. He defended himself by using his powerful muscles to swing a heavy club. He carried his burdens on his back. Then, as we have learned, man began to invent things to make work easier and life safer. Finally, in our day, almost all heavy work is done by machinery. In spite of much labor-saving machinery, we still have many uses for our muscles. Machines cannot wash our faces, dress us in the mornings or feed us. These and many other things our muscles must do for us. Muscles which are kept in good condition by proper exercise and clean living will do more work and better work than soft, weak muscles, covered with fat from the use of alcohol.

WE LEARN TO USE OUR MUSCLES

We have learned how alcohol affects the mind and what serious results come from its use. The muscles of the body are controlled by our telephone system of nerves which come from the brain. Owing to the effect of alcohol on the telephone system, we should naturally expect to find some changes in the power to use the muscles. That is just what we do find.

The human body is well supplied with muscles; in fact, it is a body of muscles. Every movement we make is controlled by the muscles, whether it is a movement of the eye, the arm, or the leg. The baby begins to crawl slowly and awkwardly at first. Then when he walks he takes many a tumble because his muscles are weak and because they are not trained. Slowly, as the baby gets older, his muscles become stronger and better trained and he learns to take better care of himself. Later in life all of us learn to make movements which require a great deal of training. We learn gradually, adding new movements as we grow older. Finally, we reach the place where we are indeed marvelous machines. We are powerful; we are fast; we are accurate; and we can do almost anything we try to do.

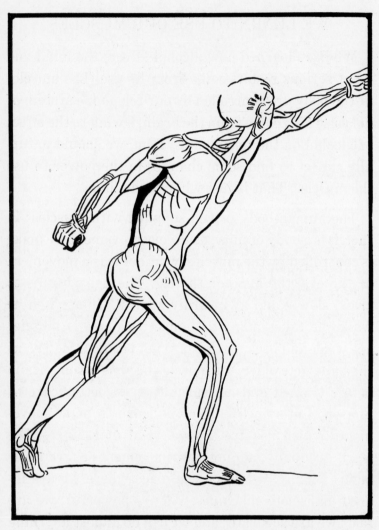

Alcohol wrecks the power, speed and accuracy of the muscles.

Most of your movements are voluntary; that is, they are movements you intend to make. You move because you wish to, and you move when you wish to. You drop a pencil and reach down to pick it up. The door is closed, you grasp the knob, turn it and open the door. You get into the car, close the door, turn the switch key, step on the starter, shift gears, and finally drive off. As you drive along you keep to the right, watching other cars so that you will not have an accident. All of these actions are voluntary. Every movement you have made was one about which you thought. Some of your movements may be made so often that you do them almost without thinking. Playing the piano is a good example of the kind of movement which becomes habit. The pianist can look away from the piano and still play correctly. All of the voluntary movements you make, you learn to do more perfectly with practice. Many of them you do without thinking. The more you play baseball, the better you can hit and catch. This is because you learn to do exactly the right thing at the right time. You learn to do things like this because your muscles have been trained to do what your brain orders.

The message comes from the brain over the proper nerves, telling the muscles what to do. Finally, the muscles of the arms and legs work so perfectly with the eyes and the rest of the body that you can hit the

Perfect timing and the use of alcohol do not go together. No one knows this better than the baseball player.

ball, or you can catch it anywhere in the field. Baseball players in the leagues call this timing. What the players mean is that the muscles are so well trained that they can, with the aid of the eyes and ears, do what the mind orders at exactly the right time. One moment too soon or one moment too late would mean a dropped ball or a struck-out batter.

ALCOHOL AND THE MUSCLES

What does alcohol have to do with the muscles? By now you know that even a small amount of alcohol affects the mind of the person who drinks it. In the

Football players cannot use alcohol and be good players.

job of "perfect timing" the brain is captain of the team, made up of nerves, muscles and eyes. The brain and eyes help the player to judge the ball. The muscles, with their speed and power, put him to the right place to catch the ball. When the ball comes down the fielder catches it, the batter is out, and the game is won by perfect timing. But suppose the fielder had taken a little alcohol between innings. His eyes would not see accurately; his mind would not be clear; and his muscles would not be able to work with the mind and eyes. Now when he goes after the ball he does not get under it soon enough and the batter is safe on first base. The player who drinks soon goes out because alcohol and perfect timing do not go together. This has been proved over and over by experience.

The football player's mind must work with his muscles and eyes. He must time his movements with the play being run. If the timing is bad, a man from the opposing team dashes through and the play is broken up. When a football team of eleven men goes out on the field, it should work together like a machine. It must have speed, power, accuracy, precision, good judgment, and the ability of every part of the machine to work together. Alcohol cuts down speed, wrecks power, destroys cooperation or the ability to work together. This is true with a football team and it is true for one man. After all, teamwork, as you have seen, is the thing which keeps the body and mind working together.

The track man, running the mile, is a team all by himself. His long graceful strides represent power, speed, accuracy, precision, good judgment, and cooperation or working together of all the muscles. To develop these things, he trains hard for many long weeks. Have you ever tried to run a mile without stopping? Well, you could not do it without a great deal of training. By training we mean eating proper food, going to bed early, living a clean life, and practicing every day on the track. Gradually, the runner improves. His wind gets better, his muscles become hard, and he has no extra fat. Now he can run the mile without stopping. Do you know what will happen to that runner if you give him small doses of alcohol every

Alcohol is the enemy of the athletes.

day while he is training? He may not look different, but put him out on the track against some well-trained runners and see what happens. He may do well the first half mile, but soon he is far behind the other runners. He becomes very tired, and, finally, has to drop out of the race.

During the Boer War in South Africa an English army of 30,000 men had to march many hundreds of miles with the greatest speed possible. There were people in danger and this army had to move quickly to save them. The weather was very hot and the water supply poor. Sir Frederick Treves was the surgeon in charge of this army which marched four months under terrible hardships. He said:

> "I was, as you know, with the relief column that moved on to Ladysmith, and, of course, it was an extremely trying time by reason of the hot weather. In that enormous column of 30,000, the first who dropped out were not the tall men, or the short men, or the big men, or little men— they were the drinkers, and they dropped out as clearly as if they had been labeled with a big "D" on their backs."

An expert mountain climber, Dr. Durig, tested the effects of alcohol on mountain climbing. He had instruments to measure exactly the amount of energy he used; how much muscle work he did; and the length of time it took him to do it. On certain days he climbed without taking alcohol, while on other days he took small amounts of alcohol before climbing. On the alcohol days he found that, while he had used a great deal more energy, it had taken much longer to climb the mountain. These tests were repeated and the results were about the same each time. Like most people who take alcohol, he probably thought, at the time, that he had done much better instead of worse.

It is interesting to know that for years Swiss mountain climbers thought the use of whiskey and wine gave them more strength for climbing high mountains. Dr. Durig proved this was wrong, and showed that a lump of sugar is worth more to the mountain climber.

The story of the English army, as well as the experiments of Dr. Durig, prove that alcohol weakens muscle power. People who use alcohol regularly are unable to last long if they are doing hard work. Neither can they stand hot sunshine. The working man who gets drunk on Saturday and Sunday does very poor work on Monday and Tuesday. He likes to sit down often, and he is so tired that he is glad to see quitting time come.

The man who drives an automobile is more likely to have an accident after taking alcohol. In the first place he drives faster than usual, but he thinks he is driving more slowly. He may think the road is straight when he is actually in a curve. Tests have been made to show that after taking alcohol, people cannot see as well. The driver may think he sees two cars coming when there is only one. His judgment is not so good in time of danger. When called upon suddenly to put on the brakes, he is slower than he would be without alcohol. We know that many wrecks on our highways are caused not only by drunken drivers, but also by drivers who have taken just enough alcohol to keep them from thinking and seeing clearly.

ALCOHOL AND THE SENSES

Our senses of sight, hearing, taste, smell, and touch are highly developed. With our eyes we can tell the difference between many colors. We can see something move, and with the aid of reason tell how fast it moves. We hear many sounds and can distinguish very fine differences between musical notes. We taste and get a great deal of pleasure out of the flavors in the foods we eat. We smell pleasant odors and enjoy them, or by being able to recognize bad odors, we can protect our health. We feel of the things in the world

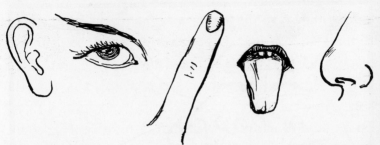

The senses of hearing, sight, touch, taste, and smell are dulled by the use of alcohol.

around us, sometimes for pleasure and sometimes for our protection. If we had none of these senses, we would be like wood or stone. Alcohol dulls and blunts every sense—sight, hearing, taste, smell, and touch. Even with small amounts of alcohol, a person is not able to see, hear, taste, smell, or feel so well as before. The drunken man looks at one car and sees two. When you speak to him you usually have to shout. His senses of taste and smell are almost completely blunted. His fingers feel numb, and he may even burn himself without noticing the pain. Often when badly injured drunken people are taken to the hospital, they do not feel pain. The doctor must wait many hours before he can ask questions to which he may get intelligent answers. Such delay may be very dangerous for the injured person.

To test the effect of alcohol on fine, skilled work, a Finnish scientist, Dr. Uno Totterman, did a needle-

Alcohol disturbs sight so much that it may cause the driver to think he sees two cars coming when there is only one.

threading test. He threaded needles, without taking alcohol, for forty-minute periods over several days. On the first day he was able to thread 103 needles, and by the fourteenth day of practice his skill had so improved that he was threading 185 needles. He then started taking alcohol in small amounts each day. He would take alcohol one day and wait until the next day to thread needles. He was able to thread 185 needles the first day but for ten days he did worse each day until he had fallen to 164 needles threaded in the test period. Further experiments always showed the same loss of skill following alcohol days.

There would be about the same loss of skill with baseball players, watch repairers, machine workers, and other people whose work requires skill and close attention.

REVIEW

1. The body is largely made up of muscles. These muscles are under the control of the brain. Most of the movements we make are intentional, that is, movements we wish to make.

2. We practice many of our intentional movements until we are able to do them almost without thinking.

3. Fine movements made with the muscles are timed by the aid of the brain, eyes, ears, and perhaps some of the other senses. This is teamwork.

4.   Alcohol disturbs the power of the brain to think, as well as to control movements of the muscles. At the same time alcohol weakens the power of the muscles to do work. The alcohol-drinking soldiers in the English army were weak and soon gave out. Dr. Durig's mountain-climbing experiments showed that even a little alcohol weakens muscle power and the ability of the muscles to do work.

5.   Alcohol dulls the senses of sight, hearing, taste, smell and touch. Dr. Totterman's needle-threading test showed that skilled muscular movements were slowed. These movements are aided by sight and touch.

QUESTIONS AND THOUGHT PROBLEMS

1.   What is a voluntary movement?

2.   How are the muscles of the body controlled?

3.   What is meant by timing? Explain just how timing is affected by alcohol.

4.   How does alcohol affect the power of the muscles of the body? Give some examples, and tell the stories connected with them.

5.   What does alcohol do to the senses? Tell about Dr. Totterman's needle-threading test, and explain what happened.

Unit X

REFLEX OR AUTOMATIC MOVE-
MENTS OF THE MUSCLES

---

1. What is a Reflex Movement?

2. How Does Alcohol Affect Reflex Movements?

3. What Happened to the Dinosaurs?

REFLEX OR AUTOMATIC MOVEMENTS OF THE MUSCLES

What a changing world we live in! Just as soon as we get used to one new thing, another one comes to take its place. The people who saw the first automobiles dashing along bumpy roads at ten miles per hour were amazed at such high speed. Now if you should try to drive on the highway at ten miles per hour a motorcycle policeman might arrest you for blocking traffic. If those first cars had been able to travel at sixty miles per hour, probably half the people would have been killed. Higher speeds came gradually and people were able to adjust themselves to the changes. When you cross the street or road you are on the lookout for cars because you have learned to do that. For thousands of years man has had to change to meet new conditions. By making such changes he has been able to survive, while animals that were unable to change no longer exist.

Our reflexes, as you will learn in this section, have a great deal to do with our protection and anything which slows or weakens reflexes also weakens that protection.

WHAT IS A REFLEX MOVEMENT?

Not all of our movements are voluntary. The brain controls voluntary movements and we are aware that we do them. Certain other movements are not directly under the control of the brain, or the will. These are known as reflex movements, and their purpose is to protect us. While most reflex movements are simple, they are very important; in fact, we could not live long without them. The centers which control such movements are not thought centers. Many of these centers are located in the spinal cord. The spinal cord is the big bundle of nerves running from the brain through a canal in the backbone. The backbone, or spinal column, is made up of short joints of bone so put together that our backs will bend when we wish to stoop over. Nerves come out from between these joints and go to all parts of the body. The spinal cord is the trunk line of nerves going to and coming from the brain.

The eye-wink is a reflex. The wink reflex protects the eye by keeping it moist and clean. Watch someone and you will see that he or she winks several times each minute. Sneezing is a reflex action and is intended to expel anything that might get into the nose. The cough reflex is to clear the breathing passages of mucus or other things that may get into them. If

you hear a loud noise near by, you will jump. This is
a reflex movement and is meant to protect you from
danger. Any reflex movement is automatic; that is, it
takes place instantly and before you have time to think.

When a baby is young, he does not think. He is controlled by reflexes. A loud noise causes him to jump.
If you brush your hand close to his face he blinks his
eyelids. He sneezes and coughs. He pulls on his bottle
for dear life. In not one of these actions has he had a
thought. He came into the world with a stock of reflexes and he uses them for his protection without
knowing one thing about what he does.

The nerve message goes to a reflex center in the
spinal cord and the response comes back instantly,
long before you would have time to think. Most important activities of the body are controlled by reflex
action. In hot and cold weather, reflex action takes
care of the size of the small blood vessels in the skin
to keep the body warm or cool. Digestive juices of the
mouth, stomach, and intestine are controlled by almost the same type of reflex action. This last is a
special kind of reflex. By its action, when you smell
food, your mouth actually waters by pouring out
saliva to moisten the food you are getting ready to
eat. At the same time, the stomach gets ready to digest the food by pouring out juices from its glands.

HOW DOES ALCOHOL AFFECT REFLEX MOVEMENTS?

All the protective reflex movements are slowed by alcohol, just as the voluntary movements are. A great many of the voluntary movements become almost reflex in their action because we do them so long we do not have to think. An experienced automobile driver does a great deal of his driving without giving it much thought. In time of danger, he puts on brakes before he has time to think. He may swing his car to one side in the flash of an eye to avoid a wreck. These are voluntary actions but they have been built up by habit until they are almost as automatic as reflex movements. Alcohol in the driver interferes with his ability to carry out the automatic or sudden actions. The alcohol may slow him up just enough to cause a serious accident.

We are living in a period which requires an ever-increasing speed in our reactions or movements. Our grandfathers lived in the horse and buggy days. Life for them was fairly simple and dangers were of a different kind. A two-day trip by horse and buggy can now be made in perhaps one hour in a fast automobile and in thirty minutes by airplane. Manufacturing plants of today, with powerful motors and high-

The use of alcohol endangers the lives of many people in this age of high-speed machines.

speed machinery have replaced the hand-worked machines of fifty years ago. On every side of us living has become more complex, and we must act quickly and accurately to fit ourselves into the changing conditions. If alcohol slows a man's movements, it endangers his life and the lives of others. He may be driving a car and have a serious accident because he is not able to judge distance, does not hear a warning, or fails to do the right thing at the right time.

Some scientists were interested in finding out how much effect alcohol has on reflex movements. By using very delicate instruments, they were able to measure the length of a reflex movement before and after alcohol was taken. One of the movements measured was the wink reflex. After alcohol was taken, the time for this movement was much longer than before. The knee-kick was also measured and showed about the same increase in time. The knee-kick is a reflex you can get by crossing your legs and having someone tap just under your knee cap. When he hits the right spot, the foot will jump forward as though it had a spring in it. These movements are slowed because the alcohol weakens the control of the nervous system over the movements. By measuring the wink reflex and the knee-kick, the scientists were able to tell how much effect alcohol has on other reflexes not easily measured. If alcohol slows the time for one reflex, then we know it slows the time for all the reflexes.

Alcohol interferes seriously with both the reflex movements and the voluntary movements. These movements are so important in piloting passenger planes, in railroading, and working with high-speed machinery, that the use of alcohol is strictly forbidden by the employers in these fields. Both kinds of movements are, of course, just as important for all other people no matter what they are doing.

WHAT HAPPENED TO THE DINOSAURS?

Do you know the story of the dinosaurs? They were huge reptiles, the biggest and most powerful creatures in the whole world. They lived long ago in the age of reptiles. So far as size and strength was concerned, they were the rulers of all living things. Some of them were as much as 80 feet in length. All other creatures were afraid of the powerful dinosaur. His thick armor protected him from his enemies. With his strength and size, he was able to destroy them. Then changes began to take place over a period of thousands of years and all living things had to adjust themselves to these changes. Speed and cunning became more useful than size and physical strength.

The dinosaur was king of the reptiles, but he lost his place under the sun because he was unable to meet new conditions.

The dinosaurs did not have much sense and were too big to be very nimble. They could not catch the smaller, smarter reptiles for food, and, of course, became fewer because they could not feed their young. Finally, all the dinosaurs disappeared from the face of the earth, and no more of their kind remained. We know that these creatures lived because their skele-

tons have been found, and many of these skeletons
may be seen in museums. The only animals that sur-
vived were the ones able to fit themselves to new conditions. The dinosaurs could not change and only
their bones are left to tell the story of how they lived.

We laugh because we think nothing like that could
happen to us. We are too fast; too intelligent. Perhaps the dinosaurs thought nothing could happen to
them because of their power, size and protection.
Sometimes we are not very intelligent. Conditions
are changing for us, but not all people are changing
with them. The ones who injure themselves by the use
of alcohol will fall by the side of life's road as they
have always done. They are the dinosaurs, neither
smart nor fast. In our day they will fall out more
quickly because the best places demand and get the
best trained minds and hands. More and more, as
time goes on, people who employ workers, demand
those who do not drink. Heavy drinkers and moderate drinkers alike are not wanted. As we shall see in
another section, alcohol, also, may have an influence
on heredity, or what our children and our children's
children will inherit from us.

REVIEW

1. Reflex movements are movements not under the control of the mind. They are much quicker than voluntary movements. The centers or places that control reflex movements are located outside the brain in the spinal cord. The eye-wink, jumping when a sudden sound is heard, and moving the finger from a hot stove are reflex movements. Reflex movements take place before we have time to think.

2. All reflex movements are slowed by small amounts of alcohol. The man who has been drinking does not jump quickly enough to keep from being hit by a car because his reflexes are slowed.

3. We are living in a machine age which, more than ever before, requires the protection of reflex movements. Accidents happen every day to people whose reflex movements have been slowed by alcohol.

QUESTIONS AND THOUGHT PROBLEMS

1. How do reflex movements differ from voluntary movements? Give examples of some important reflex movements and tell why they are important.

2. How are the reflex movements affected by alcohol? Give examples and explain as fully as you can just what happens.

3. Why is the use of alcohol more dangerous in our time than ever before? Carefully study the newspapers for one

month, and clip all news items referring to traffic accidents caused by alcohol, or traffic law violations in which alcohol played a part. Bring these to class for discussion and study.

4.   In what ways can our living conditions be compared with those of the dinosaurs?

Unit XI

HEREDITARY OR FAMILY INFLUENCE

---

1. What we Get From Our Ancestors.

2. How Alcohol May Affect the Human Race.

HEREDITARY OR FAMILY
INFLUENCE

Sometimes people inherit money from their kins-folk and think they are very fortunate. There are other things that can be inherited which few of us hear about. These things are worth more to us than money, because they may mean strong bodies, good minds, and long lives. Our ancestors pass on to us all that is strong or weak in their bodies and minds. The way these ancestors have lived for many generations may have a great deal to do with our own health. If their lives have been clean and their habits good all that we inherit from them will probably be good. Studies have been made in families for many genera-tions and these studies prove the truth of such a statement.

In this section you will be able to get an idea of how very important this kind of inheritance is to the human race.

WHAT WE GET FROM OUR ANCESTORS

People are like their ancestors, that is their parents, grandparents, and relatives even further back. They inherit their strength and their weakness of body and mind from these ancestors. Some people are intelligent because their ancestors were intelligent. Some are dull because their ancestors were dull. People are large or small; strong or weak; blue-eyed or black-eyed; smart or dull, because their parents, grandparents and great-grandparents were like that before them. We say these things are inherited, or are hereditary. What we mean is that they are passed on in the same family through many generations. Some people inherit clubfeet, cross-eyes, and certain diseases such as insanity and high blood pressure. We usually say that such things "run in families." All of you probably know of people who have some unusual troubles like those of the parents or grandparents.

The lower animals pass their good and bad points on down to their young. Plain, lazy, rabbit-running hound dogs raise the same kind of dogs. Fine dogs are raised by breeding only the strongest and smartest males and females. The finest Scotties, German shepherds, bulls and bird dogs are the results of hundreds

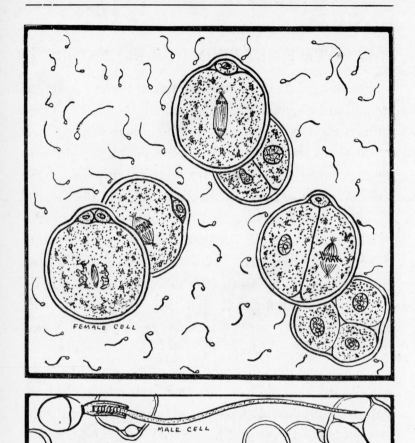

These are the male and female cells from which the young are produced.

of years of careful breeding. The first dogs were probably wild, mean and ugly. Today, dogs are our most
faithful friends, and we love them because of their
strength, intelligence and friendship.

Stock-raisers, by careful breeding, have been able to make some big improvements in cattle. As a result of carefully mating only the best animals, our prize-winning cows do not look much like their scrawny wild ancestors of a few hundred years ago.

It would be perhaps very difficult to allow only the strongest and smartest people to raise all the children. There are, however, many other ways of improving the human race. We can try to make all the people strong. Many of our habits are likely to weaken the children of the future. Bad living conditions and poor food will not grow strong boys and girls. Weak boys and girls will grow up to become the parents of weak children. If, sometime in the future, all the parents are weak, you can easily see what will happen to the human race within a few hundred years.

ALCOHOL AND THE HUMAN RACE

It is possible for bad habits to weaken our bodies and minds. This weakness may then show up in our children.

A very large percentage of the people in the world use alcohol, either in small or large amounts. Many scientists believe such a general use of alcohol by so many people can have a weakening effect on the children of the future. These scientists have studied for years to prove the truth of their belief. Experiments with people are difficult to carry on. One reason is that people live a long time, and studies running through many generations would take more than one hundred years to complete. Another reason is that the action of the alcohol would be mixed up with many other influences, such as diseases and other weakening influences.

Many studies have been made on men who had used alcohol a long time. These studies show that alcohol injures the glands which help to produce children. In a man who has not used alcohol, the cells of the glands are normal and healthy. In the man who has been drinking alcohol a long time, the cells of these glands are small and weak. A weakened gland, like a weakened person, may not be able to produce strong, healthy children. Animals were given alcohol for a long time and their glands for producing young showed the same kind of injury found in the men who had used alcohol.

Studies were made of families which had used alcohol for many years. A great many of the children born in these families were idiots, or were subject to fits, or other nervous diseases. These families were compared with other families of about the same class of people, that did not use alcohol. In the families that used alcohol almost six times as many children were thus affected. The objection to such a study is that the children may have inherited their diseases from ancestors several generations back who did not even use alcohol. Another objection is that the use of alcohol may have been the result of the inherited mental diseases in the families, rather than the cause.

Studies of inherited conditions when made on animals are better than those made with people. The reason for this is that we can get healthy animals that have been carefully bred for many generations. We know that the ancestors of these animals were free from disease. Such a study was made with dogs. One pair of dogs, a male and a female, were given alcohol every day for a long time. Out of 45 puppies born to this pair, at different times, only four puppies were healthy. Another pair of dogs of the same breed as the first pair were not given alcohol. Nearly all the puppies born to them were normal and healthy.

In other experiments of the same kind, the mother dogs that had alcohol gave birth to many dead puppies. These mothers did not have as many puppies in each litter as the mothers that had no alcohol.

Guinea pigs born to mothers that had alcohol were weaker than the baby guinea pigs of normal mothers. The bad effects showed up for several generations, in spite of the fact that only the first guinea pigs were given alcohol.

Studies made so far do not prove beyond doubt that alcohol will have effects on the race. They do seem to show, however, that this may be true. Many scientists believe that in time and with better methods for study they will be able to show that alcohol does weaken the race, and that its injurious effects may be passed on through perhaps many generations. We have every reason to think that any influence which weakens and injures people will after a time weaken the race.

REVIEW

1. People resemble their ancestral kin for many generations back of them. These resemblances may be in size, color of eyes, or brightness of mind. Sometimes people inherit defects, such as clubfeet or cross-eyes. Sometimes they inherit diseases such as high blood-pressure and insanity.

2. Animals can be improved by breeding, that is, by mating only the best males and females.

3. The use of alcohol weakens the bodies and minds of people who use it. Many scientists believe that such weakness may be passed on to the children of parents who use alcohol.

4. Studies made in families that had used alcohol for years showed that a great many of the children were idiots and had certain nervous diseases.

5: Studies were made with animals which had been given alcohol for a long time. The young born to these animals were weaker than the young born to normal animals. In some of the animals the weakening effects of the alcohol showed up for several generations, although only the animals of the first generation had alcohol.

QUESTIONS AND THOUGHT PROBLEMS

1. What is meant by ancestors, and by inheritance? Give examples of inheritance in your own family.

2. Make a careful study of how some animals you know about are improved by breeding.

3. How do you think the use of alcohol might affect the human race in the future? Give some reasons for your opinion.

4. How can we best study the effects of alcohol on inheritance?

5. Can you think of any other influences that might weaken the human race?

6. From your own experience and from what you have read, make a list of things you think might help to make people healthier and stronger.

Unit XII

ALCOHOL AND THE BODY'S RESISTANCE TO DISEASE

---

1. How the Body Resists Disease.

2. Alcohol Weakens the Power of the Body to Resist Disease.

3. Alcohol Causes Disease.

149

ALCOHOL AND THE BODY'S RESISTANCE TO DISEASE

Good health is just about the finest thing in the world. We cannot help being sick sometimes, but we can have less sickness than any other people who have yet lived in the world. It is no longer necessary for half the people in any country or city to die in one epidemic or outbreak of disease. Do you know why? Because we can be vaccinated for many dangerous diseases. Modern sewer systems take care of your wastes, your water is made pure before it reaches you. If you do not live in the city, your parents are more careful about wastes, drinking water, and food than ever before. You have been surrounded by all the safeguards of modern medicine and good health laws. We can have all these, however, and still weaken our bodies in many ways so that diseases may easily attack us. You will be able to learn in Section Twelve how people can weaken the resistance of their bodies to disease.

No matter how little we are sick, we think we have been sick too much. No matter how long we live, we think the time is too short. By making it our business to have good health, we can live better and longer.

HOW THE BODY RESISTS DISEASE

Many people live for years without being sick. Do you know why? The best answer we have is that a healthy body can usually drive away or destroy the disease germs that try to get in. There are at least four ways in which our bodies may do this.

1. All of you know what happens after people have measles, mumps, chickenpox, whooping-cough, smallpox, and typhoid fever, as well as some other diseases. We can say that if you have any of these diseases once and get well you will probably never have them again. There is a good reason for this. The body, in its fight to overcome any one of the diseases, forms something which is kept in the blood and cells to prevent a second attack of that disease. The white blood corpuscles or cells which we will learn about in this section, also help in the work of protecting the body.

2. The scientists in their laboratories have found a second way to keep us from having some of the diseases such as diphtheria, scarlet fever, typhoid fever and smallpox. All of you have been vaccinated for smallpox and typhoid. When you were younger most of you probably had the vaccination for diphtheria and scarlet fever. If all people were vaccinated, there could be no smallpox, no typhoid fever, no diphtheria,

and no scarlet fever. In the past years before vaccination was known these diseases killed hundreds of thousands of people.

3. The third type of protection is not so good as the other two. This is a natural power the body has to help us resist diseases. Sometimes when one member of a family has a disease which is contagious or "catching" as we say, other people in the same house may not have the disease. This natural power the body has to help us keep free from diseases depends largely on good health. It is not the same kind of protection we get from vaccination, or from an attack of measles or mumps.

The natural resistance of the body may be weakened by exposure to wet, cold weather. It may be weakened by a poor diet, as well as a lack of exercise and a run-down condition of the body. People who work long hours without enough sleep and rest are weakened and usually do not have much resistance to disease.

Nearly all of us have tuberculosis germs in our lungs. When our bodies are in good condition, these germs are held as prisoners and may do no harm. If the body's resistance is weakened, the tuberculosis germs can begin growing and soon one may have tuberculosis.

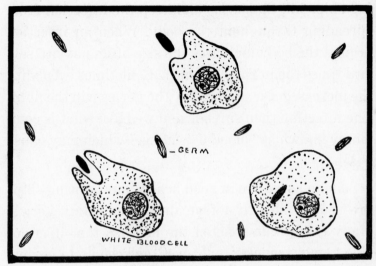

The white blood cells help to defend the body against disease by capturing and killing germs. In the picture the white cells can be seen taking in some of the germs.

4. Do you know that you have a real navy of fighting ships in your body? Your fighting ships are the white blood corpuscles (kôr'-pŭs-ls). These tiny ships are in the blood and they can actually move under their own power to any part of the body where enemy disease germs threaten to get in. A good example of how the fighting ships move is shown in their attack on a boil. A boil is caused by germs which get through the skin. When the boil comes to a head, it is full of pus. The pus is made up of millions and millions of the little fighting ships. Each one has captured and killed many germs. By surrounding the boil, the fight-

ing ships kill the germs and keep the infection from spreading throughout the body. When an infection occurs, the body increases the size of its navy to several times the normal strength. Sometimes even with the increased size of the navy the germs win the fight. The infection then spreads and we have what is commonly known as "blood poisoning," which may cause death.

So long as we are in good health, our fighting ships are usually able to defeat and kill invading germs. Many things can weaken the navy so that it is not able to move quickly, fight well, or keep up to normal strength.

ALCOHOL WEAKENS THE POWER OF THE BODY TO RESIST DISEASE

The defenses of the body against disease are weakened by the use of alcohol. By weakening the body, alcohol weakens the natural defenses of the body against disease. People who use alcohol neglect their health and expose themselves to disease. Because the natural defenses are weakened, alcohol users get diseases more easily than people who do not use alcohol. The white blood cells, or the fighting ships, are not able to do their best in people who drink alcohol. Such people get infections more easily, and it takes them longer to recover from wounds or injuries. We do not know how the alcohol affects the white blood cells, but we do know it keeps them from fighting as they should.

Studies have been made with both people and animals which prove that the body's power to resist diseases is weakened by the use of alcohol. It has been found that drinkers get sick with pneumonia much more easily than people who do not use alcohol. Experiments with animals show the same thing. One group of animals was given alcohol every day for a period of time. These animals were then exposed to the germs which cause pneumonia. Many of them had pneumonia and died. Another group of animals which had no alcohol was exposed to pneumonia germs in the same way. Only a few of these animals came down with pneumonia, and a very small number of them died.

Studies were made with people who had been using alcohol regularly for a long time. When such people became sick with pneumonia, a great many more of them died than was the case of the pneumonia patients who had never used alcohol. Out of each one hundred alcoholic people who had pneumonia, almost fifty died. Out of each one hundred who had never used alcohol and who had pneumonia, only twenty-five

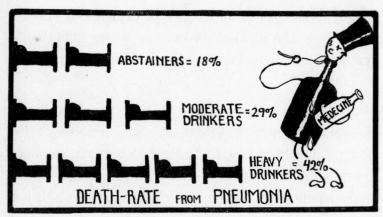

This chart shows the difference between the death rate from pneumonia, in abstainers or people who do not drink, in the moderate drinkers, and in the heavy drinkers.

died. So you can see that the regular alcohol drinkers have only half as many chances to get well from pneumonia as those who have never used alcohol.

Alcohol weakens the resistance of the body to tuberculosis. Those people who have been using alcohol a long time seem to get tuberculosis more easily than the ones who have never used alcohol. In certain countries where most of the people have used alcohol daily for long periods, it has been shown that tuberculosis is more common than in the countries where alcohol is not used so much. This has been proved by experiment. Tuberculous animals to which alcohol was given died ten per cent sooner than animals with the same disease that had no alcohol.

For every three thin people who reach the age of seventy only one fat person will reach the same age.

In cholera, a disease of the tropics, ninety out of every one hundred people who used alcohol, died from the disease, but only nineteen out of every hundred died out of the group that had never used alcohol.

Certain other studies seem to show that the alcohol users do not recover as soon from injuries as the people who do not use alcohol. Wounds of the alcohol users become infected more easily because of weakened resistance. A larger percentage of them die from injuries.

A good many other diseases are more common in people who use alcohol. Gout, a condition which affects the joints and especially the joint of the great toe, is usually thought to be due almost entirely to the use of alcohol.

As we have already learned, beer tends to increase body fat. To a smaller degree, this is also true for all alcoholic drinks. People, whether fat from the use of alcohol or from other causes, have poor disease resistance. For every three thin people who reach the age of seventy years, only one or two fat people will reach the age of seventy. The fat people cannot move around so well, they take very little exercise and, of course, are not in good physical condition.

HOW ALCOHOL CAUSES SOME DISEASES

In Boston, Massachusetts, studies have been made which show that alcohol may cause certain diseases by weakening the body. The scientists making these studies have been able to show that alcohol will bring on certain diseases, which are caused by poor diet. People who drink are able to live on alcohol for several days at a time. When this happens, these people do not eat a balanced diet. Soon they become ill with what we call deficiency diseases. By deficiency disease is meant a disease caused by a deficient or poorly balanced diet. One of these diseases, pellagra, is common in the Southern States. Two other such diseases are beri-beri and scurvy.

You drink fruit juices and milk, eat vegetables such as cabbage, lettuce, and sometimes take cod liver oil, to keep from having the deficiency diseases. In the fruit juices, milk, vegetables, lean meat, and cod liver oil, you get substances known as vitamins which prevent such diseases. These vitamins along with the necessary fats, carbohydrates and proteins make up a balanced diet.

The Boston scientists have shown that heavy alcohol drinkers usually live on a poorly balanced diet which does not contain enough vitamins. The absence of these vitamins from the diet brings on the deficiency diseases.

REVIEW

1. The human body is protected against diseases in four ways:

> (a) Some diseases we rarely ever have a second time. The germs which cause any one of these diseases vaccinate our bodies at the time we have the disease.

> (b) Vaccines may be made from typhoid, diphtheria and other germs. When properly used, these vaccines prevent the diseases for which they are used.

(c) We are protected to some extent from diseases by good health. A weakened body is less able to resist diseases. A weakened body is also less likely to recover from diseases.

(d) The white blood corpuscles imprison and kill disease germs to prevent disease. They also help to fight diseases after we become sick.

2. Alcohol weakens the natural defenses of the body against diseases. The white blood corpuscles are weakened and cannot do their best work.

3. People who use alcohol get pneumonia easily and they are more likely to die from it than pneumonia patients who have not used alcohol. The death rate from cholera is much higher among the drinkers than among the non-drinkers.

4. Many alcohol users do not eat properly and as a result may develop diseases because of a lack of some of the vitamins.

QUESTIONS AND THOUGHT PROBLEMS

1. Explain what you think is meant by the body's resistance to disease.

2. What are the four ways you have of protecting your body against disease?

3. Make a list of the diseases for which you can have protection either by vaccination or from having had the diseases.

4. Do you think alcohol weakens the power of the body to resist diseases? Give reasons for your belief.

Unit XIII

HOW LONG WE LIVE

---

1. Does Alcohol Shorten Life?

2. Records of Insurance Companies.

HOW LONG WE LIVE

You have learned that people inherit the strength and weakness of their ancestors. In addition to inheritance, we have another influence that has much to do with good health and long life. In some ways our bodies can be compared to automobiles. An automobile in the hands of a careful person may run for ten years. To make an automobile last for such a long time, it must be driven carefully and have proper attention. Many cars are good for only a year or two because they are in the hands of careless owners.

The human body is built to last much longer than an automobile. Our bodies are less likely to need repairs and more likely to last well for seventy years if we give them intelligent care. Many people do not seem to know how important it is to give their bodies this care. As a result, they are often sick and wear out long before they should. If all people were very careful about diet, exercise, health, and the use of harmful substances, such as alcohol, the average length of human life could be increased by at least a dozen years.

DOES ALCOHOL SHORTEN LIFE?

Sometimes stories are told about men who live to be a hundred years old, even though they have used alcohol most of their lives. People who say alcohol is not harmful to the body tell such stories to prove their own belief. They do not tell us about the people who use alcohol a long time and die from its effects many years before they should die.

We have learned in an earlier section that alcohol weakens the power of the body to resist, or keep off certain diseases. Future studies may show that the same thing is true for other diseases. We have also learned that people who use alcohol do not have as good chance to get well from certain diseases as people who have never used it.

We know that people who become drunk are more likely to get wet and cold in bad weather; they have lost the power to reason and do not know enough to take care of themselves. Such people get sick more easily because they expose themselves, and because (as we know already) their bodies are not so well able to resist disease germs as the bodies of people who do not drink. Again people who use alcohol are more likely to get killed by falls, or by automobiles, and machinery. They cannot see, hear or walk well and the thinking part of their brains is numb so that they cannot protect themselves.

For many years we have wanted to know whether alcohol shortens the lives of people who use it. Everybody knows that the ones who take alcohol in large amounts have much shorter lives than those who never drink. We are more interested in what happens to the people called the moderate drinkers; that is, the ones who drink alcohol every day, but in small amounts. They do not get drunk, and perhaps by looking at them we could not tell that they are in anyway different from the people who never drink. If we had records of how every person had lived and died in the last hundred years, we could study these records and find what we wish to know. Unfortunately, no complete records of this kind have ever been kept. Such records would be easy to keep and perhaps will be kept in the future. Until a few years ago, no records of births and deaths were kept. Now, when a baby is born, a birth certificate must be made. When someone dies, a death certificate must be made before the body can be buried. These certificates are kept in the State Department of Public Health, and from them many valuable studies can be made.

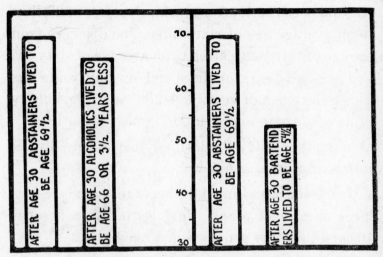

AFTER AGE 30 ABSTAINERS LIVED TO BE AGE 69½

AFTER AGE 30 ALCOHOLICS LIVED TO BE AGE 66 OR 3½ YEARS LESS

AFTER AGE 30 ABSTAINERS LIVED TO BE AGE 69½

AFTER AGE 30 BARTENDERS LIVED TO BE AGE 54½

Insurance charts show that the abstainers or the people who do not drink are the ones who live longest.

RECORDS OF INSURANCE COMPANIES

The only records we have on how alcohol affects the length of human life are those of the life insurance companies. They are the records of people who had life insurance in the companies. Several different studies have been made, though none of them are very complete, and the information is not as accurate as we would like it.

In one study all the people were put in two groups. One group included all who were known to have used alcohol; and the other group included those who had never used it. It was found that the abstainers (those who did not drink), after reaching the age of 35, lived to an average age of sixty-nine. The drinkers from the age of thirty-five, lived to an average of sixty-five and one-half years, or three and one-half years less. Three and one-half years does not seem long, but few of us would care to give up that much of our lives.

In another study the insured people were divided into four groups as follows:

Group one represented the average death rate for a large number of people. This death rate was set at 100 and the other groups compared with it.

Group two represented the moderate drinkers who used two glasses of beer or one glass of whiskey daily. In this group the death rate was 118, or eighteen per cent higher than in group one.

Group three represented people who had once been regular drinkers but who had quit. Their death rate was 150, or fifty per cent higher than group one. This seems to show that even after these people quit drinking, enough injury still remained to shorten their lives.

Group four represented the people who drank about two ounces of whiskey daily. Their death rate was 186, or eighty-six per cent higher than group one.

Another study was made on people who were drunk two or three times each year, and each time stayed

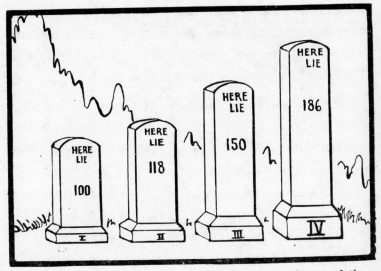

The death rate of the drinkers is higher than the death rate of those who do not drink.

drunk two or three days. The death rate in this group was very high. The death rate from pneumonia was three and one-half times higher than normal; kidney disease, four and one-half times the normal; brain hemorrhage, four times the normal; heart disease, three times the normal.

In England studies were made among people who worked with beverage alcohol—some manufacturing it, some selling it in saloons and hotels. These people were compared with others working at different occupations. It was found that after reaching the age of thirty, the people who worked with alcohol lived as much as fifteen years less than the people in the other occupations. The reason they had such short lives was, of course, due to the fact that they could drink alcohol any time they wanted it.

Experiments made on animals have shown that many of the new-born of alcoholic mothers are dead at birth. The ones that live are weaker and less likely to grow up. In human mothers who use alcohol it is well known that many of the babies are born dead, and many of the ones that are alive at birth do not live long. This is about what we should expect. A healthy, careful mother will usually bear healthy children, who have a good chance of growing into manhood and womanhood. The mother who uses alcohol will hardly pay as much attention to her own health or try to be in good physical condition for the birth of the babies. It is not likely that she will care for her children as well after they are born.

We have still not found an answer to how small amounts of alcohol effect the length of life. What one person would consider small amounts of alcohol might be enough to affect the length of life. It is doubtful if more than a few people who use alcohol, take it in the amounts small enough to have no injurious effects. Usually if they begin by drinking small amounts of alcohol, most people gradually increase these amounts until they are harmful.

In studies such as the ones made by the life insurance companies, people who are questioned will not always tell the truth about how much they actually drink. Some of the people classed as moderate drinkers, are really heavy drinkers. It seems reasonable to think that few of the people who call themselves moderate drinkers, actually continue to remain moderate drinkers. The longer people drink the more they are able to drink without becoming drunk. Although they use rather large amounts of alcohol, they still call themselves moderate drinkers. Many people say moderate drinking has never hurt anyone. In the first place there are few moderate drinkers who stay moderate. In the second place there is more proof that moderate drinking is harmful than that it is not harmful.

REVIEW

1. Do the moderate drinkers of alcohol live as long as the people who do not drink it?

The insurance companies have tried to answer this question by comparing groups of drinkers with groups of non-drinkers. Their studies show that after the age of 35 the lives of the drinkers are three and one-half years shorter than the lives of the non-drinkers.

Another study showed that moderate drinkers have a death rate eighteen per cent higher than normal; the regular drinkers who had quit drinking had a death rate fifty per cent higher than normal; and the heavy drinkers had a death rate eighty-six per cent higher than normal. Other studies showed that the drinkers have higher death rates than normal for pneumonia, kidney disease, brain hemorrhage, and heart disease.

2. Experiments with animals have shown that many newborn young of mothers given alcohol were dead at birth.

3. In human mothers who use alcohol many of the babies are born dead and many of the ones that live are not strong babies.

4. People who call themselves moderate drinkers have always thought their drinking would not hurt them. All the studies that have been made seem to prove that alcohol shortens the lives of the moderate drinkers.

5. It is also true that the people who drank alcohol for years and then quit using it do not live as long as they should.

QUESTIONS AND THOUGHT PROBLEMS

1. Make a list of things you think people should do to have good health and long lives. Some of these things you will find in the text, and some you can get from what you already know.

2. In how many different ways can alcohol affect the length of life in the people who use it?

3. How does the action of alcohol in people who use it, endanger the lives of other people?

Unit XIV

ALCOHOL INJURES SOCIAL HEALTH

---

1. We Cannot Live to Ourselves.

2. The Social Drinkers.

3. Insanity, Crime and Accidents.

ALCOHOL INJURES SOCIAL HEALTH

How about the other fellow? Of course, you could say, "every fellow for himself." Even if you were so selfish, that would be a poor rule. If you were on an island all by yourself, life would soon become very lonely. When you live in a community with other people, you must consider their safety and welfare in the things you do. The man who uses alcohol does not do this, because he is not able to think or to control his actions. He may endanger the safety of many people and he is often responsible for the loss of other people's lives.

WE CANNOT LIVE TO OURSELVES

In our country today conditions that weaken the health of the individual may affect the lives of many people. Over the years our living conditions have changed a great deal. There was a time when sick people were nursed by their neighbors. Then as time went on and population increased, the job of caring for the sick became too big for the neighbors. Hospitals were built by the largest communities and charitable institutions were set up to care for the aged and the poor. Gradually this obligation passed from the community to the counties, cities and states. Finally the Federal government stepped in to help carry the burden. These changes have taken place because communities, towns, cities and states have become more closely connected by good roads and rapid transportation.

There was a time when each community produced its own food, made its own clothing, and many of the people lived and died in a community without ever traveling fifty miles from home. Now we buy what we need from other states and countries. We ship our own products to other places in exchange for what we buy. We travel to other states to visit or to live, and the people from other states visit us or come to live among us. These changes in living have created social problems which affect not one but many communities. The community across the river which did not affect us a few years ago, has now become a part of our community. We are no longer cut off from that community by the river and a lack of transportation. Its schools are our schools; its roads are our roads; its problems are our problems, and its diseases may easily become our diseases.

Alcohol affects every person in every community, whether he uses it or not. Individuals can no longer say: "What I do is nobody's business but my own." Under a new social order that statement must be replaced by: "What I do may be my own business, but I must remember that whatever I do affects other people." Alcohol, as you have learned, not only weakens the resistance of the body to disease, but it causes disease, and it shortens life. Its effects may possibly be passed on indirectly to future generations to weaken the people of those generations. While all this is going on, medical science battles to give people more happiness through better health and greater length of life. The fight against disease and the things that cause disease has just begun. All of us can help in that fight by learning what harmful substances do to our bodies and by using that knowledge to keep good health.

THE SOCIAL DRINKERS

There has grown up in our country within the past few years a practice called "social drinking." The social drinkers get together in the evenings to chat over their cocktails or alcoholic beverages. They pride themselves with the fact that their drinking comes only after the day's work is done. From the effects of the alcohol, they feel very comfortable and become merry and talkative. Often one drink calls for another and still another, until everybody is mildly intoxicated. In their homes, alcoholic beverages are always kept, and when friends drop in, alcoholic beverages are usually served. At their social functions alcoholic beverages take the place of harmless refreshments. Social drinking is a daily habit among millions of people in our country. The insurance companies rate the social drinkers as steady drinkers. Their death rate is probably high. Their disease-resisting power is weakened. Their mental and physical ability to do work is lowered.

INSANITY, CRIME AND ACCIDENTS

Insanity.—In a study of the effects of alcohol on the human race, we must study the effects of alcohol on the human body. Our dogs, our cattle, and our horses are pedigreed or registered, that is there are records

Alcohol increases the flow of people through these gates.

of them going back for many generations. People are not pedigreed, and we have no records of what our ancestors were. When we try to study the influence of alcohol in insanity, we are not very successful. We know that alcohol causes insanity, but we do not know how great the percentage is; and we do not know what inherited defects are present along with alcohol to cause insanity. Sometimes we may go so far as to say the inherited defects of the mind caused the weakness and the desire for alcohol. We are certain that a good percentage of alcoholic insanity cases are due to the effects of alcohol and not to other causes. It is estimated that between ten and fifteen per cent of the insane people in asylums are there because of alcohol.

Crime.—Our prisons hold many people whose crimes are due to alcohol. Some estimates have been made that one-fourth of all the people in prisons are there due to alcohol. Since no records are kept as to how people live, there is no way to make a true esti-

How many wrecks are caused by alcohol?

mate on what percentage of crime is caused by alcohol. It must be high. The cost of all crime is said to run above twelve billions of dollars yearly. If one-fourth of all crime is caused by alcohol, the alcohol part of crime cost would run to four billions of dollars, enough money to pay for health education and health training for every person in the United States.

Accidents.—In the United States, during the year 1935, 36,000 people died in automobile accidents, and 1,000,000 were injured, many crippled for life. Ten per cent of these deaths and injuries have been credited to alcohol. This does not tell the whole story. If we gave alcohol credit for between one-fourth and one-half of the accidents, we would probably be nearer correct. The numbers given in these figures were only for the ones caused by people who were drunk. The ones who had only a few drinks, but enough to cause an accident, were not credited to alcohol.

REVIEW

1. Over a period of less than fifty years communities have become closely tied together. Diseases may be spread easily because people are able to travel from one community to another more readily. Our highways are filled with automobiles and every driver must know not only how to drive but he must be in good condition for driving. If drivers are drunk, or have been drinking, they make the highways dangerous for other people. Many drinkers still feel that it is nobody's business how much they drink. In a society such as our own, anything we do affects other people.

2. The social drinkers are the people who get together in the evening to drink and talk. They belong in the group classed by the insurance companies as moderate drinkers. This means they will have a higher death rate than normal.

3. Alcohol causes diseases of the mind and a certain percentage of people in insane asylums are there because of alcohol.

4. Alcohol causes some of the crime and many people are in prison because of crime.

5. The use of alcohol increases automobile and industrial accidents.

QUESTIONS AND THOUGHT PROBLEMS

1. Criticize the expression, "what I do is nobody's business but my own."

2. Make a list of the ways in which your own actions can affect the welfare of other people.

3. What are some of the dangers of social drinking?

Unit XV

HABIT-FORMING DRUGS AND PAIN-RELIEVING REMEDIES

———

1. Narcotic Drugs.

    A. Opium (Morphine and Heroin).

    B. Cocaine.

    C. Hashish.

2. Pain-Relieving, Sleep-Producing Drugs.

HABIT-FORMING DRUGS AND PAIN-RELIEVING REMEDIES

Psychologists (sī-kŏl'ŏ-jĭsts) are scientists who study the growth, powers, and functions of the human mind. One of them has said that each person is a bundle of habits. Some of these habits are good and some are bad. Habit is an important word for all of us and we use it a great deal. We are interested here in substances called habit-forming drugs. These drugs have a peculiar effect on the minds of people who use them. Once the drug habit is formed, it is difficult and sometimes impossible to break. It often results in complete loss of the physical and mental power of the user. Many people who use habit-forming drugs were not normal to begin with.

Even normal people easily fall into the habit of taking other drugs which we call pain-relieving remedies. These drugs are so common that all of you know about their use if not their danger. In Unit Fifteen of this book you will learn about the danger of habit-forming drugs, as well as pain-relieving remedies.

NARCOTIC DRUGS

A narcotic is any drug which produces sleep or stupor and at the same time relieves pain.

Alcohol is, of course, a narcotic substance, but is usually studied in a class by itself.

The narcotics are called habit-forming drugs. People begin taking these drugs to relieve pain, such as headache, toothache, or rheumatism. The pain is stopped and they are able to rest and sleep. This may happen many times, and finally these people cannot sleep well without the drug, even when there is no pain. Then they use the drug not to relieve pain, but as an easy way of getting to sleep. Gradually, as their bodies get used to having sleep-producing drugs, the people become nervous and ill-tempered without them. This is the beginning of a habit which soon grows so strong that will power is weakened and the person is no longer able to control his wishes. He now takes the drug because he cannot do without it. We call these people drug addicts. An addict is a person who gives himself up to a drug habit which he is unable to quit.

Only a few years ago, even the most dangerous narcotic drugs could be bought by everyone. Our own national government in Washington saw the rapidly increasing number of people who were beginning to use narcotic drugs. A Federal law was passed which allows the manufacture and sale of these drugs only by licensed manufacturers and druggists. Such drugs can be used only for treatment of sick people by doctors having a Federal license.

Violation of this law is a serious offense and may be punished by a prison sentence. All the other nations of the world have seen the danger from the use of narcotic drugs and they, too, carefully control the production and sale of these drugs. The League of Nations, which is a congress made up of nearly all the countries of the world, has agreed on plans to prevent the unlawful shipment of narcotic drugs from countries where they are produced. Such laws and regulations have greatly cut down the number of people using narcotics.

Even with our narcotic laws in effect, and enforced by a small army of Federal officers, the sale of narcotic drugs is still a serious problem. The drugs are smuggled, or sneaked in from countries where they are produced. People who have the drug habit will pay almost any price for narcotic drugs. This will show you what a powerful influence such drugs have.

A. OPIUM (Morphine and Heroin)

Opium is the oldest and most widely used of all narcotic drugs. It is the most powerful and most dangerous of all the narcotics. For this reason the Federal government at Washington controls the sale and use of opium in this country. Before opium was put under Federal control, it could be bought by anyone who wanted it, and in this country alone a half-million or more people were opium addicts. In certain parts of the world, as Asia, where opium is produced, about one-fourth of all the people were addicts. With control enforced by the governments of these countries, the use of opium has been greatly reduced.

Opium comes from the poppy plant which is grown mainly in China and India. In these, as well as other countries, poppies are cultivated to produce opium. After the petals of the poppy flower wither, a seed capsule or pod is formed. When this capsule is split with a knife, a white milky juice flows from the cut. As the milk comes out, it hardens and is scraped off and collected. The gummy substance when dried is known as raw opium. Opium is the crude, or raw drug, that is, the drug which has not been purified. From the crude opium come at least twenty purified drugs. The most important ones are morphine, codeine, and heroin.

These are known as the alkaloids (ăl-kā'-loids) and are the things in opium which make it have its narcotic action on the brain. When we speak of the action of opium, we mean the combined actions of all the alkaloids found in opium. The main difference between the actions of the alkaloids is the difference in their strength. Some of them have a weak action, while others, like morphine and heroin, have a powerful action. When we speak of opium, we may mean opium or morphine, because both have the same kind of action.

Opium is one of the oldest drugs known to man. Its medical and narcotic powers have been used since the beginning of history. Opium was probably first produced in India and in modern times introduced into China, though we usually think of it as a Chinese drug.

When opium is given by your doctor it is one of the most valuable of all medical drugs. It is the only substance known to man which will completely relieve pain. It does this by numbing the nerve telephones which carry pain messages to the brain. No pain messages can get through to the brain. In many diseases, the sick people have so much pain they cannot rest or sleep. If this keeps up for a few days, they are completely worn out and, of course, will not get bet-

*Chinese opium addict getting ready to smoke his opium pipe.
He lies down to smoke. In the lower part of the
picture are some poppy flowers.*

ter. In some conditions pain may be so bad that the sick person will have convulsions or spasms and may die. When opium, in the form of morphine, is given, it stops the pain and gives the sick person a chance to rest and sleep. With such rest he will be refreshed and the cells of his body may be able to do their work better.

Certain diseases like cancer cannot be cured after they have gone too far. In some of these conditions pain becomes so severe that the patients cannot get a moment's rest or sleep. With opium or morphine properly given they can be kept from suffering for many months.

Unlike alcohol, opium (morphine) has a most useful place in the treatment of sick people. Until something is found to take its place, opium (morphine) will still be one of the six most valuable drugs we have for the treatment of disease.

It is unfortunate that such a valuable drug as opium (morphine) should have any bad uses. It is estimated that in the United States over 100,000 people are opium (morphine) addicts. These people take morphine because it gives them a pleasant dream-like feeling. They forget all of their troubles and seem to live in an imaginary world in which there is no pain or worry. Before a long while, the addict cannot get along without morphine. If it is suddenly taken away from him, he becomes nervous and excited. He sweats a great deal, gets weak and has cramps in his abdomen. Finally, he becomes wild with excitement and if some morphine is not given to him, he may die.

If the habit is continued, the morphine addict takes larger doses of the drug. He soon becomes selfish and ill-humored. He is careless about his clothes and appearance. He will not tell the truth and will not keep his word. He is sulky and suspicious so that he does not like to be with people who are his friends. Later he becomes forgetful and does not remember things. His mind becomes weak, and, finally, there is a complete loss of mental power. Beginning later, other changes take place. There is a loss of appetite; the muscles become weak; and there is loss of weight, until finally the addict looks like a walking skeleton. His skin becomes hard and dry and hot with fever. His eyes are sunken and he does not look at people. Sexual power is lost. His digestive system is upset and he stays badly constipated.

Before this stage is reached, the mental p.   are weakened and the addict may have to be p.   an asylum.

Opium and morphine are taken in three ways. Opium is smoked in pipes like tobacco. This meth.

This is a hop house where opium addicts go to smoke opium. The Chinese letters by the side of the door spell, "OPIUM SHOP."

is used mainly by the Chinese. Regular opium houses are kept with pipes and rooms for the addict. In these places, called hop houses, he smokes and goes under the influence of the drug. In this condition he dreams of riches he will never have and beauty which will not be his. When he awakens everything is gone except the misery of weakness and fear. (2) Morphine tablets are taken by mouth but most addicts do not like this method. Morphine is bitter and does not taste good. It also upsets digestion when it gets to the stomach and intestines. (3) The addict usually takes morphine by injecting it under his skin with a hypodermic needle, such as the ones you see in the doctor's office.

Heroin (hĕr'ō-ĭn) is another drug which comes from the raw opium It is more dangerous than either opium or morphine. Heroin is so dangerous that the Federal government will not allow it to be brought into this country. It is more rapid in its effects than opium or morphine. Drug addicts like heroin because it can be snuffed up the nose where it is absorbed by the mucous membrane into the body. Heroin addicts are more likely to commit crimes and they become insane much sooner than opium or morphine addicts.

B. COCAINE (kō′kȧ-ĭn)

Cocaine is a drug which comes from the coca plant. The coca plant is grown in South America and has been known since the earliest visits of the Spanish explorers in Peru. It is now grown largely in Bolivia.

Cocaine has only one use as a medical drug. It is a local anesthetic. We saw how ether is used to put people to sleep so that the entire body is benumbed and cannot feel pain. Cocaine can be used to put one finger to sleep without affecting the other parts of the body. What happens is that when the cocaine dissolved in water is injected around the nerves of the finger, these nerves can no longer carry pain messages. The finger is numb, or as you say, it is asleep. A surgeon can cut into the finger without hurting the person. Cocaine can be sprayed into the nose or throat and will benumb the mucous membranes so that the doctor can work without hurting his patient. Better local anesthetics, however, have been discovered and have almost taken the place of cocaine.

Cocaine is also a habit-forming drug. Cocaine addicts are called "snowbirds." Cocaine is a white flaky substance and looks very much like light snow flakes. The addict snuffs the white flakes of cocaine up his nose where it is absorbed by the mucous lining of the

This is the way cocaine was used as an anesthetic to stop pain. The coca plant is seen in the lower part of the picture.

nose. It is then carried to the cells of the body by the blood. Some drugs such as liniments and salves when rubbed into the skin are absorbed into the body in the same way. Many drugs which will not pass through the thick skin, may very easily pass through the thin moist mucous lining of the nose and mouth. Cocaine will give the same effects when injected under the skin with a hypodermic needle.

When taken by snowbirds, or addicts, cocaine acts much more quickly than opium or morphine. The cocaine addict gets pleasant dream-like effects from the drug. He soon loses his appetite and his digestion is upset. He becomes pale and nervous. He may lose as much as fifty pounds within a few weeks. His muscles become weak and his hands tremble. His eyes are sunken and he cannot sleep at night. The snowbird, or addict, may have ulcers or sore places in his nose from snuffing the cocaine. Gradually, he becomes mentally and morally weak. He sees bugs crawling and thinks he feels worms creeping under his skin. He imagines people are trying to kill him and he may rush out to commit robbery and murder. Finally, he becomes completely insane.

Cocaine weakens the body so that it is easy for the addict to get diseases. Most of the addicts soon die from the effects of the cocaine, but those who live a year or two longer usually die from other diseases. One out of five cocaine addicts who live will have tuberculosis.

Cocaine, like opium and morphine, is under the control of the Federal government. It is one of the most dangerous of the narcotic drugs and its sale is carefully controlled.

C. HASHISH (Indian Cannabis) (Mariahuana)

Cannabis is also known as Indian hemp and hashish and Mariahuana (măh-rĕ-ah-wȧh'nȧh). It comes from the flowering tops of the Indian hemp plant. The drug is seldom used as a medicine. Its only interest then comes from its narcotic effects. It has become a very dangerous narcotic drug in the United States during the past ten years. The reason for this is that the hemp plant can be grown in the United States. We have always known, of course, that the plant could be grown anywhere. We thought, however, that only the Indian hemp grown in India and Mexico, contained the active narcotic of cannabis. Now we know that Indian hemp grown in many sections of the United States is just as powerful as hemp plants grown in India and Mexico.

The hashish addict gets his effect from the drug by smoking the dried flowering tops of the hemp plant.

Soon after smoking he begins to feel very light and imagines himself to be in the midst of beautiful gardens. Ideas pass through his mind so fast that he cannot remember them. He seems to be in a world of happiness where no trouble or pain can come in. Time has no end and space is lost. The addict is the center of a world of beauty and everything in it belongs to him. All sense of judgment and reason is lost. It is said that a Persian chief who was fighting against the Crusaders gave hashish to his body guards. The guards always became so crazed that they would draw their swords and rush madly out to kill the Crusaders. These people called the drug haschisch and the killers were called hashshashins (hash-shas-hins). From this came our word assasin, which means a person who sneaks up and kills someone.

Hashish or cannabis acts only on the brain and nerves. At first the person is very much excited. He sees the visions as we have learned. Following this he cannot walk, and finally he falls into a drunken sleep. After a person uses hashish for only a few months his eyelids become red and swollen. He is weak and becomes tired very easily. His appetite is poor and he does not sleep well. Before a great while he has difficulty in remembering things. From this time on, his mind becomes weaker and soon he is

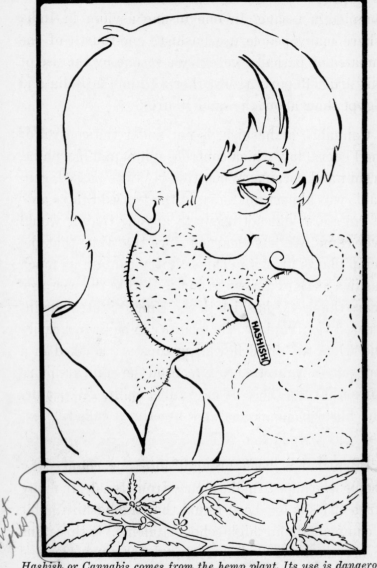

Hashish or Cannabis comes from the hemp plant. Its use is dangerous and may cause insanity. The hemp plant is shown in the lower part of the picture.

completely insane. In one insane asylum in India
where many people use hashish, one-fourth of the
inmates or patients were made insane by the use of
this drug. Reports from other asylums in India and
Egypt show about the same figures.

Cannabis, or hashish, is not under the control of
the Federal law which controls opium and morphine,
heroin and cocaine. When this law was passed, cannabis was almost unknown in the United States and,
of course, it did not occur to anyone that it would
ever come. We have learned since that time that the
hemp plants grown in this country contain as much
hashish as those grown in India. Within the past few
years the use of hashish in the United States has increased very rapidly. The plants can be grown easily
and when the dried flowering tops are smoked in a
pipe or as a cigarette, the effects on the mind are more
powerful than those of morphine, opium or cocaine.
The hashish cigarettes are sometimes called "reef-
ers."

Hashish has been brought into our country by
people who hope to make money from its sale. In many
large cities it has been found that the hashish habit
is common among high-school students. It threatens
to become more widespread and dangerous by far
than any of the other habit-forming drugs. In many

states and cities laws have been passed in an attempt to stop the spread of this dangerous drug.

PAIN-RELIEVING, SLEEP-PRODUCING DRUGS

In the United States a few years ago, the use of narcotic drugs was a serious problem. Then, as you have learned, the Federal government passed laws to limit the sale and use of such drugs. These laws have been so well enforced that the danger from opium and cocaine is fairly well under control. Without such laws, we should probably have millions of drug addicts in our country today instead of around 100,000.

One hundred years ago, people lived quietly, without hurry or worry. In those days there were no good roads; automobiles and airplanes had not been thought of. Then came the time when people had these things and more.

Now we have so much to do and so many places to go that we have very little time for rest or play. We rush around all the time. We gobble our food and get indigestion. We work hard and become nervous. We stay up late at night and do not get enough sleep. Finally, we have headaches; we worry; we are nervous, and we cannot sleep. Do you know what a great many people do when they are in this condition? They will not stop to rest; so, they take something to make them feel better, or they take something to make them sleep. At first the remedy may be aspirin, luminal, acetanilid, bromide, or veronal tablets. Soon it is two, three and more tablets. After a time, this becomes a habit and the person thinks he cannot get along without his tablets. He carries them during the day and keeps them by his bed at night. An occasional tablet is not dangerous, but the habit which means taking them several times each day or night is dangerous.

The pain-relieving, sleep-producing drugs can be bought everywhere. Their over-use may produce serious injury to health and may even cause death. It is well known that some of these remedies can destroy the white blood corpuscles which form the body's navy of defense against germs. When disease germs attack the body, millions of these white corpuscles rush in to kill and destroy the attacking germs. If there are not enough white corpuscles, a sore throat, boil or other infection will spread germs throughout the body and death may result. The red blood corpuscles, which carry oxygen to the cells of the body, may also be injured. When this happens the cells do not get enough oxygen and the skin becomes blue.

Aspirin, when taken for a long time, may cause weakness of muscles, difficulty in seeing, delirium and injury to the heart. Some people cannot take even small doses of aspirin because it gives them a swelling of the face and throat and makes them very weak. Aspirin is especially dangerous for children who are often poisoned by small doses. It is, however, the least dangerous of all the pain-relieving remedies.

Veronal and luminal may cause mental depression, a feeling of fear, and weakness of muscles. The continued use of these drugs may cause increased weakness, loss of judgment, loss of memory, disturbance of speech, difficulty in seeing, with injury to the eyes, pains around the heart, dizziness and loss of appetite.

Acetanilid may cause weakness, loss of appetite, loss of weight, anemia or pale skin, and heart failure. Even in doses of three or four tablets acetanilid may show signs of poisoning.

Any of the pain-relieving, sleep-producing drugs may irritate and injure the stomach. It has been estimated that cancer causes from ten to twelve per cent of all deaths. It is not surprising that nearly half of all cancers found in the body occur in the stomach. Many men who have spent much time trying to find the cause and cure for cancer, believe that among the causes for cancer of the stomach may be listed the irritation and injury from the continued use of alcohol, pain-relieving drugs, tobacco, tea, coffee and hot foods.

The pain-relieving, sleep-producing drugs are not powerful habit-forming drugs. Such drugs are dangerous because they are easy to get and because millions of people in our country use them. Even the school boys and girls are falling into the habit of using these drugs.

Just remember that any drug habit is a poor master and a false friend. Remember, too, that pain is the warning cry of sick cells. A pain-relieving drug only covers up the pain, without curing the cause. Sometimes that cause may be eyes that need glasses, an infected sinus, the beginning of a serious disease, a tired mind begging for rest, or a sluggish body that needs exercise.

REVIEW

1. A narcotic is a drug which causes sleep and relieves pain. The narcotics are habit-forming drugs. Their use is so dangerous that their sale in this country is controlled by our Federal government.

2. Opium is the oldest of the narcotic drugs. It comes from the poppy plant. From the raw opium are obtained more than twenty drugs, each having somewhat the same action.

3. The opium drugs are among the most valuable of all medical drugs.

4. Opium is used as a habit-drug by smoking it in a pipe. Morphine tablets are usually dissolved in water to be injected under the skin through a hypodermic needle. Heroin is the most dangerous of the habit-drugs. It cannot be legally brought into this country.

5. Cocaine comes from the coca plant grown in South America. Cocaine addicts sniff the fluffy cocaine powder up their noses where it is absorbed by the mucous membrane. Sometimes cocaine is used by injecting it under the skin.

6. Indian cannabis (hashish, mariahuana) is grown mainly in India and Mexico, though we know now it may be grown in any warm climate. The flowering tops of the plant are dried and smoked in pipes or cigarettes by the addicts.

7. All of the narcotic drugs—opium, morphine, cocaine and hashish are dangerous habit-forming drugs and for the user may result in insanity and finally death.

8. The pain-relieving, sleep-producing drugs, such as aspirin, luminal, acetanilid, bromides and veronal, may become habit-drugs though they are not so powerful as the narcotics. Millions of people get into the habit of taking them to relieve pain or to produce sleep. Their use finally becomes a habit which is dangerous to health.

9. Such drugs may produce a number of different types of injury in the body, and some of them may weaken the mind. Finally they may cause insanity and death.

10. The pain-relieving remedies are made more dangerous by the fact that anyone can buy them, and because people who use them do not know that they are dangerous to health.

QUESTIONS AND THOUGHT PROBLEMS

1. What is a narcotic drug?

2. When can narcotic drugs be of great value and when can their use be very dangerous to health and life?

3. You have probably never seen a drug addict. Can you explain why this is true?

4. Why do people fall easily into the habit of taking pain-relieving remedies?

5. How can the use of all habit-forming drugs become dangerous?

Unit XVI

CONCLUSION

You are completing the study of alcohol and the habit-forming drugs. In the first section you saw alcohol as a very useful substance, having a high value in the industrial arts, chemistry and the hospital. Next came the story of how alcohol, once considered very highly as a medicine, was largely dropped from use because all the studies showed it had little value. Then there followed the discussion of the effects of alcohol in the stomach, small intestine, cells, heart and blood vessels. In the brain you saw the most important effect of alcohol. Here there is a loss of thinking power as well as the ability to learn and remember.

Muscle power and fine muscular movements are interfered with, depending on the amount of alcohol taken. The senses of sight, hearing, tasting, smelling and feeling are dulled. The reflexes are slowed so that a person is unable to respond quickly to things that might endanger his life.

The ability of the body to fight off disease as well as to recover from disease is weakened by alcohol. This is shown by the fact that alcohol users not only get pneumonia more easily but a larger percentage of them die from the disease. In the next section the result of weakened resistance to disease is seen in failure of alcohol users to live as long as those who do not use it. Every insurance study shows that all people who drink will be expected to die sooner than those people who do not drink. This loss in length of life varies from two or three years for the moderate alcohol drinkers to as much as ten or fifteen years for the heavy drinkers.

The social influence of alcohol is closely tied up with its effects on the body. Whatever affects one must affect the other both for the present and the future. After all, the social health of a nation is just as important as its physical health, and is closely related to it.

In the section on habit-forming drugs and the pain-relieving remedies you learned how easily people form the habit of taking drugs. Finally, they are bound so completely by such habits that it is difficult or impossible to break away from them. The danger to health and life from these habit-drugs is a fact no one would attempt to deny.

In this study of alcohol and the habit-forming drugs an attempt has been made to give you the truth in a way that would be both interesting and helpful. In past years people in general have known little about the effects of alcohol and habit-forming drugs on the body. They were perhaps honest in their belief that such substances are not harmful. This book brings to you information which older people did not have. Its only aim is to help you make intelligent decisions when the time comes to make them. If that aim is accomplished, it will have fulfilled its purpose in rendering to you a good service.

SUGGESTED AIDS FOR THE TEACHER

PALMER: *A Syllabus in Alcohol Education*
> 50 pages. A logical organization of the several steps in the study of alcohol—source, nature, actions, uses outside the body and effects when taken in drinks, showing the relation between these several phases. Arranged pedagogically for teachers and others who need an orderly understanding of the subject. Easy reading, high-school vocabulary. What every teacher should know about alcohol, regardless of the grade she will teach. 25 cents, $13.00 per 100.

WILLIAMS AND STODDARD: *The Scientist Experiments With Alcohol*
> 50 pages. Descriptions of thirteen experiments performed in seven different countries, showing effects of alcohol on muscular control, endurance, hearing, mental control, color perception, typewriting, etc. For teachers of all grades and for high-school reading. 25 cents each, $13.00 per 100.

MEDICAL RESEARCH COUNCIL: *Alcohol: Its Action On the Human Organism*
170 pages. Eleven chapters. By the British Medical Research Council, appointed to report the effects of alcohol for the benefit of Parliament in making laws to control sales. 50 cents.

U. S. TREASURY (Bureau of Industrial Alcohol, Washington, D. C.) : *The Uses of Alcohol as an Essential Chemical in the Arts, Sciences and Industries*
50 pages. Explains why ethyl alcohol is used in the arts, sciences and industries. Interesting information everyone should know about "a modern miracle." 10 cents each.

Order from The Signal Press, Evanston, Illinois

The Foundation for Narcotics Research and Information, Inc., 150 Fifth Avenue, New York, N. Y., maintains a free library and information service, available, without charge, to schools, educators, and students.

HAVEN EMERSON, M.D.: *Alcohol and Man.* A Source Book on the Effects of Alcohol on Man in Health and Disease. 450 pages, $3.50. Macmillan Company, New York City.

SCIENCE WORD LIST

The science word list will be helpful in giving a better understanding of words not in common use. All of the words in this list have been used one or more times in the different sections of the book.

KEY TO SOUNDS

ā as in āte.
â as in car′bon-âte.
â as in câre.
ă as in ăm.
ä as in ärm.
ȧ as in ȧsk.
ē as in ēve.

ė as in ėvent.′
ĕ as in ĕnd.
ē as in moth′ēr.
ī as in īce.
ĭ as in ĭll.
ō as in ōld.
ô as in ôbey.

ô as in ôr′der.
ŏ as in ŏdd.
ōō as in fōōd.
ū as in ūse.
û as in ûnité.
û as in bûrn.
ŭ as in ŭp.

Abdomen (ăb-dō′mĕn). The part of the belly containing the stomach and bowels.

Acetanilid (ăs-ĕt-ăn-ĭl-ĭd). A white powder used in certain of the pain-relieving remedies.

Accurate (ăk′ů-rȧt). Careful, true, exact.

Addict (ă-dĭkt′). A person who gives himself up to a drug habit.

Air sac. The tiny thin-walled sacs in the lungs. The lungs are almost completely made up of these air sacs.

Alcohol (ăl′kȯ-hōl). A colorless liquid which is the part of whiskey, wine and beer that causes the drinker to become drunk.

Alkaloid (ăl′kȧ-loid). The substance in a drug which gives the drug its action. Some drugs may contain more than one alkaloid as in the case of opium.

Ammonia (ȧ-mō-nĭȧ). A strong smelling gas dissolved in water, and is made up of hydrogen and nitrogen.

Ancestors (ăn′-sĕs-tēr). Kinsfolk, as grandparents or great-grandparents from whom we are descended.

Ancients (ān′-shĕnts). Usually means the people who lived in the oldest periods of civilization, or even before civilization began.

Anesthetic (ăn-ĕs-thĕt′-ĭk). A substance such as ether, used to produce a deep sleep and a loss of pain sensations.

Antiseptic (ăn′tĭ-sĕp-tĭk). Anything that will prevent or destroy the growth of bacteria.

Artery (är-tēr-ĭ). A blood vessel going away from the heart to carry food, oxygen and water to the cells of the body.

Asp (ȧsp). A small poisonous snake of Egypt and near-by countries.

Aspirin (ăs′-pĭ-rĭn). A mild pain-relieving remedy.

Automatic (ô'tô-măt'-ĭk). Self-acting; not voluntary; not depending on the control of the will.

Bacteria (băk-tē'-rĭ-à). Microscopic living plants. Some of them cause disease and are called germs.

Beri beri (bĕrĭ'-bĕrĭ'). A disease of the nerves caused by the absence of vitamins from the diet.

Beverage (bĕv'-ēr-àj). A drink.

Birth Certificate. A record of the birth of any baby. This record must be turned in to the State Health Department, where it is kept.

Boisterous (bôis'-tēr-ŭs). Rough, rude, noisy.

Brain. The part of the nervous system enclosed inside the skull.

Breed (brēd). To produce young.

Bromide (brō'-mīd). A drug to quiet nervousness and cause sleep.

Cannabis (kăn'-ăb-ĭs). A dangerous narcotic drug which comes from the flowering tops of the Indian hemp plant. It also is known as hashish and mariahuana.

Carbohydrate (kàr-bō-hi'-drāt). The starch and sugar foods which come largely from plants.

Carbon Dioxide (kär'-bŏn dī-ok'-sīd). A heavy, colorless, odorless gas. Plants use carbon dioxide in the same way animals use oxygen.

Carnage (kär'-nàj). Great loss of life; slaughter.

Cat Gut. Sheep gut cut into fine threads to be used by surgeons in sewing up wounds.

Centigrade (sĕn'tĭ-grād). A thermometer having 100 divisions or degrees from 0 to 100 so that zero degree is the freezing point, and 100 degrees the boiling point of water. This is the chemical thermometer used in the laboratory.

Cholera (kŏl'ēr-ä). A disease most common to warm climates. The signs are, vomiting, diarrhea, and cramps in region of the abdomen.

Circulatory System (sûr'-kŭ-là-tô'rĭ). The heart, arteries, capillaries and veins taken together to make up a complete system.

Clubfoot. A condition in which a child is born with badly-shaped feet.

Cocaine (kō'kà-ĭn). A drug used to deaden pain, also a dangerous habit-forming drug.

Cocktail. An alcoholic drink to which flavoring substances have been added.

Conscious (kŏn'-shŭs). To know what is going on around one. When a person faints he is not conscious.

Constipation (kŏn'stĭ-pā'-shŭn). A disturbance of the bowels in which there is difficulty in getting rid of the body waste materials from the intestines.

Contagious (cŏn-tā'-jŭs). A contagious disease is one that may be passed from one person to another.

Contract (kŏn-trăkt'). To get sick with some kind of disease, as to contract pneumonia.

Corpuscle (kôr'-pŭs-l). A blood cell; as a white or red corpuscle.

Cooperation (kô-ŏpēr-ā'shun). The act of working together in a pleasant way.

Cross-Eyes. A condition in which the eyes look in toward the nose, due to weak or short eye muscles.

Crusader. Once meant a soldier in any of the military expeditions which tried to take the Holy Land from the Mohammedans. Now means also one who undertakes anything with zeal and enthusiasm.

Deaden. To cause to have a dead feeling; as to blunt a feeling to pain.

Death Rate. The percentage of people dying each year as compared to the total living population.

Degree. A division as on a thermometer divided into 100 degrees.

Depressant (dė-prĕs'-ănt). A drug which lowers or slows any activity of the body.

Destructive. Anything which tends to destroy or ruin.

Digestion (dĭ-jĕs'chun). The process of breaking down food in the stomach and intestine so that it may be used by the cells of the body.

Digestive Juices. The juices poured out by the glands of the mouth, stomach and intestine. These juices have the power to digest or break down food.

Dinosaur (dī'nô-sôr). A class of reptiles which have been extinct for many thousands of years. They varied in length from 2 to 70 feet.

Diphtheria (dĭf-thē'rĭ-ȧ). A disease caused by germs which may grow in the throat and manufacture a poison which will injure the cells of the body.

Disease (dĭ-zēz'). Sickness resulting usually from the growth of germs in the body. Some diseases are not caused by germs.

Distillation (dĭs'tĭ-lā shŭn). The process of heating a liquid so that the steam goes off into a coiled tube. The outside of the tube is cooled by running water so that the steam inside the tube is changed back into liquid to be collected as it runs out.

Drug. Any substance obtained from animals or plants, used as a medicine.

Epidemic (ĕp'-ĭ-dĕm-ĭk). The spread of a disease among many people of one or more communities, as an epidemic of influenza.

Elastic. Any material, such as rubber, that can be stretched and will then return to its original shape and size.

Ether. A chemical substance used to put patients to sleep for operations. It is made by distilling alcohol with sulfuric acid.

Experiment (ĕx-pĕr'ĭ-mĕnt). A test run in the laboratory in an attempt to prove something or to learn something new.

Extinct (ĕks-tĭnkt'). Any thing that may have lived in the past but does not any longer exist.

Fahrenheit (fä'rĕn-hīt). A thermometer scale named after its maker, G. D. Fahrenheit. He made the scale so that 32 degrees above zero is the freezing point of water, and 212 degrees above zero is the boiling point of water. This is the weather thermometer seen in almost every home.

Fat. Animal cells made up of greasy or oily tissue, as fat meat. Fats are found in both animals and plants.

Ferment (fĕr'-mĕnt). Anything that will cause fermentation, as the ferment made by yeast cells. Fermentation causes milk to sour, breaks down fats, carbohydrates, and proteins in the stomach and intestine. Each process is caused by a different ferment.

Fermentation (fûr′měn-tā′shŭn). The chemical changes caused by the action of the ferments. An example of this is formation of alcohol by the action of yeast ferment on sugar water.

Generation (jĕnēr-ā shŭn′). The average lifetime of a man, about 70 years.

Germ (jûrm). Tiny plant or animal cells too small to be seen except through a microscope. Many diseases are caused by germs.

Germicide (jûr′mĭ-sīd). Any substance such as carbolic acid or alcohol, which will kill germs.

Gland. An organ of the body which secretes or pours out some useful fluid. The glands of the mouth, stomach and intestines pour digestive juices to digest food.

Gout (gout). A condition in which there is swelling and pain in some of the joints of the body, especially of the great toe.

Hemorrhage (hěm′ŏ-rǎj). The escape of blood from a wounded or broken blood vessel.

Heredity (hê-rĕdĭ′-tĭ). The act of passing from parent to child certain characteristics, as blue eyes, red hair, size, or intelligence. Defects may be passed along in the same way.

Herdsman. One who tends to herds of cattle or sheep.

Infection (ĭn-fěk′-shŭn). The growth of germs in the body to cause either disease or injury. A wound may become infected, but is still not a disease.

Inflammation (ĭn′flă mā′-shŭn). Redness and swelling with heat and pain in any part of the body. Usually caused by an infection or growth of germs.

Inject (ĭn-jěkt′). To put in or under, as to inject a drug under the skin.

Injurious (ĭn-jōōrĭ-ŭs). Any thing that is harmful to the body.

Irritate (ĭr′ĭ-tāt). To cause mild injury to any tissue of the body, as from rubbing or from the use of some chemical substance.

Insanity (ĭn-săn′ĭtĭ). A condition in which the mind is not normal. Insane people do not know right from wrong, and may become dangerous.

Intestine (ĭn-těs′-tĭn). The long, narrow tube in the abdomen which receives food from the stomach. It helps in the process of digestion and is more than 30 feet in length.

Joint. Any part of the body where two bones come together so as to allow motion.

Kidney (kĭd′-nĭ). One of a pair of organs located below the stomach, in front of and on either side of the backbone.

Mad Stone. A stone taken from the gall bladder of a deer. It was supposed to stick to the wound made by the mad dog's teeth, and to prevent hydrophobia.

Malt (môlt). Grain, generally barley, soaked in water until it germinates or sprouts. It is then dried and used in making beer.

Mariahuana (măh-rĕ-ah-wâh′năh). Another name for cannabis, hashish or Indian hemp.

Mental (měn′tăl). Concerning the mind or intelligence.

Mental Depression. The act of weakening or dulling the mind. Alcohol produces mental depression.

Microscope (mī′krŏ-skōp). An instrument which magnifies objects too small to be seen by the natural eye.

Mineral (mĭn′ẽr-ăl). A substance, as iron, dug from the ground. Minerals are found in small amounts in some foods and water. They are necessary for the needs of the body.

Morphine (môr-fĭn). A habit-forming drug which comes from opium. It is also a valuable drug in treatment of disease.

Mucous membrance (mū′kus mĕm-brăn). The lining of any passage or cavity of the body, as the mouth, stomach, intestines, nose, or lungs.

Museum (mû-zē′ŭm). A laboratory or place where specimens are preserved for study and for the interest of people who care to see them.

Narcotic (när-kŏt′-ĭk). A drug which in small doses relieves pain and induces sleep.

Nausea (nâ′shê-à). A feeling of sickness at the stomach with a desire to vomit.

Nerve (nŭrv). One of the white fibres which connects the brain with other parts of the body to carry messages.

Nervous System (nŭr′vŭs sĭs′tĕm). The brain and all the nerves of the body thought of as a telephone system.

Numb. Without feeling, somewhat as a sensation of a foot or hand asleep.

Oxygen (ŏk′-sĭ-jĕn). A colorless, odorless, tasteless gas found free in the air. It makes up about 21 per cent of the air, and is necessary for all animal life.

Paralyze (păr′à-līz). To take away the power to move. When a leg or arm is paralyzed it cannot be moved by its own muscles, because the nerves are injured and cannot carry messages to and from the brain.

Patent Medicine. Any medicine or remedy made by a secret formula which is not made known to the public, and which was not worked out and tested by scientific people.

Pellagra (pĕ-lăg′rà). A disease caused by a lack of vitamin G in the diet.

Pneumonia (nŭ-mō′nĭ-ă). A serious disease of the lungs affecting the entire body and often causing death. One attack does not protect the body against attacks of the same disease later on.

Poison (poi′-zn). Any substance which when applied to or taken into the body is harmful to the cells of the body.

Precision (prê-sĭzh′-un). The quality of being accurate or exact.

Prescribe (prê-skrĭb′). The act of a doctor in writing an order for medicine to be given to a patient. The order may be for treatment other than by the use of medicine, as rest, sunshine, or certain forms of exercise. A prescription is always the written order of the doctor.

Reaction. A response.

Reflex. A movement not under the control of the will.

Resistance (rê-zĭs′-tăns). The power of the body to keep free from disease.

Salve (sălv). Medicine dissolved in an oily substance, such as vaseline or lanolin (oil from sheep wool).

Sewer (sū′ẽr). A pipe line to carry away waste materials.

Scientist (sī'ĕn-tĭst). A person who is learned in science, and who makes studies in the laboratory to learn new things.

Sluggish (slug'-ĭsh). Dull; drowsy; slow; not very active.

Smallpox (smôl'-pŏks'). A contagious disease in which the body is covered with eruptions or sores. When healed, these eruptions usually leave small hole-like scars in the skin.

Solvent (sŏl'-vĕnt). A liquid such as alcohol or water in which solid materials may be dissolved.

Specimen (spĕs'-ĭ-mĕn). A sample or one out of a group to show what the other members of the group are like.

Spinal (spīnăl). Referring to the spinal column or backbone.

Spree (sprē). A person who stays drunk for several days is usually said to have been on a spree.

Sprout. To begin to grow, as seeds sprouting.

Sterilize (stĕr'ĭ-līz). To kill bacteria either by the use of chemicals or heat.

Stimulant (stĭm'ū-lănt). Any drug or substance which produces increased activity of the cells of the body.

Stupor (stū-pŭr). A loss of consciousness, either partial or complete.

Surgeon (sûr'jŭn). A doctor who operates on patients.

Sweat (swĕt). The moisture poured out through the pores of the skin by the sweat glands.

Symbol (sĭm'bŏl). A sign by which a thing is known. Words are sound symbols. Letters are sign symbols.

Temperature (tĕm'pĕr-à-tûr). Degrees of heat.

Thermometer (thĕr-mŏm'ê-tĕr). An instrument for measuring heat.

Tradesman (trādz-măn). Usually a shopkeeper or one who sells.

Unconscious (ŭn-kŏn'shŭs). A condition caused by disease or injury in which a person is not aware of what is going on around him. A fainting person is unconscious.

Veronal (ve'rôn-ăl). A pain-relieving remedy.

Vaccination (văk-sĭn-ā'shŭn). The process of protecting people from smallpox. Now we usually use the word vaccination to cover most forms of produced disease protection.

Vomit (vŏm'ĭt). To throw food up from the stomach.

Voluntary (vŏl'ŭn-tĕr'ĭ). Any act of choice, that is, anything we do because we wish to do it.

Vitamins (vī'tà-mĭnz). Substances in food necessary for growth and good health.

Zoology (zo-ŏl'o-gy). The study of animal structure.

INDEX